Sue Barley

D0222622

Paragraph
Patterns

Paragraph Patterns

Barbara Auerbach   Beth Snyder
Brooklyn College of the City University of New York

HARCOURT BRACE JOVANOVICH, PUBLISHERS
San Diego   New York   Chicago   Austin
London   Sydney   Toronto

About the Cover: Stairwell of the old lighthouse at Cabrillo National Monument, located atop Point Loma in San Diego, California. © 1981 Barbara Martin/Los Angeles Times Photo.

Copyright © 1983 by Harcourt Brace Jovanovich, Inc.

All rights reserved. No part of this publication may be reproduced or transmitted in any form or by any means, electronic or mechanical, including photocopy, recording, or any information storage and retrieval system, without permission in writing from the publisher.

Although for mechanical reasons all pages of this publication are perforated, only those pages imprinted with an HBJ copyright notice are intended for removal.

Requests for permission to make copies of any part of the work should be mailed to: Permissions, Harcourt Brace Jovanovich, Publishers, 757 Third Avenue, New York, NY 10017.

ISBN: 0-15-567983-X
Library of Congress Catalog Card Number: 82-084562
Printed in the United States of America

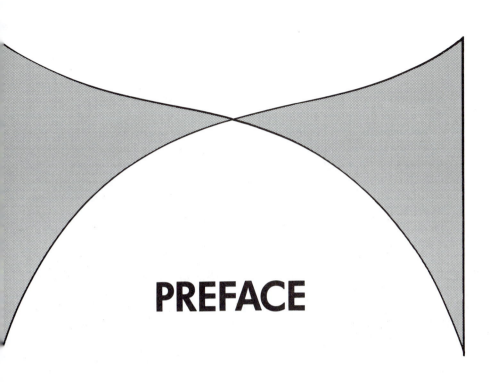

PREFACE

Paragraph Patterns is an intermediate writing text for students of English as a second language in universities, language institutes, and adult education programs. All reading passages, exercises, and writing tasks focus on the paragraph while presenting and developing a variety of rhetorical modes: description, narration, generalizations and specifics, classification, cause and effect, problem solving, comparison and contrast, and personal opinion.

The first chapter begins with a definition and description of the paragraph and its three parts: the introduction, discussion, and conclusion. Writing tasks that ask students to recognize the topic sentence and later to produce an appropriate topic sentence are stressed in this chapter. This chapter sets the groundwork for the rest of the text and is essential for the students' successful performance in subsequent chapters.

As well as focusing on various rhetorical modes, Chapters 2 through 11 have specific themes of interest. The thematic topic is introduced in the Prewriting Strategies section by questions that generate involvement with the topic. Useful content vocabulary accompanies these questions and is later found in the reading selection. The reading selection expands on the theme and exemplifies the rhetorical mode of the chapter. Following the reading are discussion questions that encourage students to relate their personal experiences and opinions to the topic.

The Writing Exercises section begins by presenting vocabulary that will help students structure their paragraphs in a specific rhetorical mode. The four organization exercises that follow the structure vocabulary require analytical and/or productive skills. In addition to emphasizing a particular rhetorical mode, each chapter treats an aspect of paragraph development: topic sentences, unity, completeness, or coherence. A sentence combining and a proofreading exercise complete this section.

These exercises are grouped so that when students have completed the entire Writing Exercises section they can tear it out and hand it in.

The chapter concludes with a Formal Writing section. The writing topics require students to use the specific rhetorical mode when developing their paragraphs, and a checklist follows to help the students proofread their paragraphs, before handing them in for evaluation.

As teachers of writing, we strongly believe that students must be motivated to communicate their ideas in writing. Too many texts stress the mechanics of writing without stimulating the students' imagination. We have strived to make the thematic content in *Paragraph Patterns* meaningful and challenging to students of different cultures and to develop the students' writing skills with varied and effective exercises.

BARBARA AUERBACH

BETH SNYDER

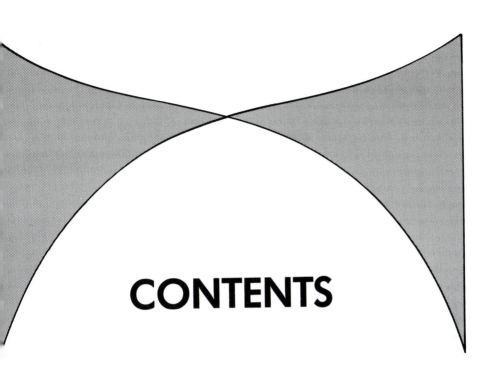

CONTENTS

3

NARRATION   25

4

GENERALIZATIONS AND SPECIFICS   37

5

PERSONAL OPINION   51

6

CLASSIFICATION 67

7

COMPARISON AND CONTRAST 79

8

CAUSE AND EFFECT 93

9
PROBLEM-SOLUTION   107

10
COMPARISON AND CONTRAST   119

11
PERSONAL OPINION   133

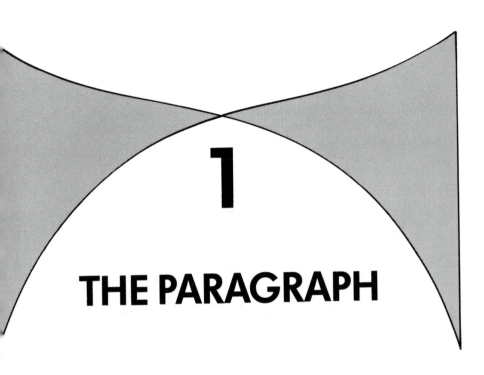

THE PARAGRAPH

DESCRIPTION

A paragraph is a group of related sentences that develops one dominating idea. A paragraph is complete alone, but it can also be part of an essay or a chapter in a book. This diagram shows the relationship of the parts that compose a book.

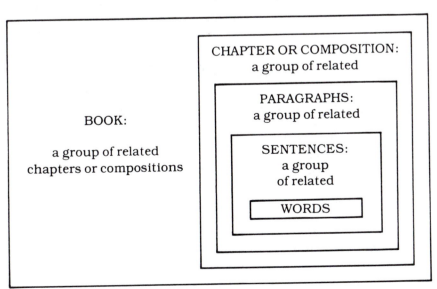

BOOK:

a group of related
chapters or compositions

CHAPTER OR COMPOSITION:
a group of related

PARAGRAPHS:
a group of related

SENTENCES:
a group
of related

WORDS

All paragraphs begin with an empty space known as indentation. Indentation signals the start of a new paragraph, and each paragraph has only one indentation. This is how a paragraph should look:

Xxxxxxxxxxxxxxxxxxxxxxxxxxxxxxxxxxxxxxxxxxxxx
xxxxx. Xxxxxxxxxxxxxxxxxxxxxxxxxxxxxxxxxxxxxxxx
xxxxxxxxxxxxxxxxxxxxxxxxxxxxxxxxxxxxxxxx. Xxxxx
xxxxxxxxxxxxxxxxxxxxxxxxxxxxx. Xxxxxxxxxxxxxxxxx
xxxxxxxxxxxxxxxxxxxxxxxxxxxxxxxxxxxxxx. Xxxxxxxxx
xxxxxxxxxxxxxxxxxxxxxxxxxxxxxxxxxxxxxxxxxxx. Xxxx
xxxxxxxxxx. Xxxxxxxxxxxxxxxxxxxxxxxxxxxxxxxxxxxx
xxxxxxxxxxxxxxxxxxxxxxxxxxxxxxxxxx. Xxxxxxxxxxxx
xxxxx. Xxxxxxxxxxxxxxxxxxxxxxxxxxxxxxxxxxxxxxxxxx
xxxxxxxxxxxxxxxx.

There is no rule for how long a paragraph should be. The length depends on the central idea that is developed. Some ideas take longer to express and develop than others because of the amount of supporting details. Nevertheless, every paragraph must adequately develop its main idea without introducing too many new ideas which should have paragraphs of their own. Each paragraph must focus on a certain topic and develop an idea concerning that topic.

Just as the length of a paragraph varies, so does its organization. The organization, like the length, depends on what the writer wants to communicate to the reader. You will practice different kinds of organization that fulfill different needs.

ORGANIZATION

The Three Parts of a Paragraph

Most paragraphs are composed of three parts; we will call them the *introduction, discussion,* and *conclusion.* In the introduction the writer tells the reader what he is going to discuss. This is conveyed by a *topic sentence.* The topic sentence expresses the main idea concerning the topic of the paragraph. (Note: The topic sentence is not always stated in the introduction; sometimes it is part of the discussion or conclusion. Sometimes it is *not* stated, and the reader must infer the main idea from the discussion. However, for now we will be practicing the introductory topic sentence.)

TOPIC: Society's responsibility toward the individual

TOPIC SENTENCE: Society is responsible to a certain degree for
                        the well-being of the individual.

The middle part, or the *discussion,* is the longest section of the
paragraph because it contains explanatory and supporting details
that relate to the topic sentence in the introduction.

DETAILS: opportunity for work
               education and training
               individual's contributions to society

The writer chooses details to elaborate the idea about the topic
and organizes them in a logical pattern.

THE PARAGRAPH SO FAR:

> Society is responsible to a certain degree for the well-
> being of the individual. For example, all people should
> have the opportunity to work and support themselves. So-
> ciety should also give individuals an education that will
> prepare them for a profession. Then, as productive
> human beings they can make the society they live in
> better.

The *conclusion* completes the discussion and frequently refers
to the main idea expressed at the beginning of the paragraph. Sometimes the conclusion is a restatement of the topic sentence; sometimes it summarizes the details in the discussion. The conclusion,
similar to the introduction, is not very long. One or two sentences
are usually enough.

CONCLUSION: By encouraging people to fulfill their own ambi-
                  tions, a society grows stronger and more produc-
                  tive as a whole.

THE COMPLETED PARAGRAPH:

> Society is responsible to a certain degree for the well-
> being of the individual. For example, all people should
> have the opportunity to work and support themselves. So-
> ciety should also give individuals an education that will
> prepare them for a profession. Then, as productive

human beings they can make the society they live in better. By encouraging all people to fulfill their ambitions, a society grows stronger and more productive as a whole.

The Proportion of the Three Parts of the Paragraph

The paragraph is a construction built with three parts, and these parts should have correct proportions (lengths). The introduction and conclusion are shorter than the discussion in the middle.

Introduction: topic sentence

Discussion: details that support
                  and explain the topic sentence

Conclusion: summary or restatement

Writing Task 1

Study this example of a paragraph having good proportion and indicate the three different parts with parentheses (   ). Notice the length of each section.

Because my brother and I have very different personalities and interests, it is sometimes hard to believe we are related. My brother, Jim, is extremely friendly and outgoing. He likes to spend all of his free time with friends, whereas I need a lot of privacy and enjoy being by myself. In addition, while I have enjoyed school since I was a child, Jim has never liked school. He prefers working at a job and being very active physically. I actually think I could be happy being a student all my life. In spite of our differences Jim and I are close friends as well as brothers.

Writing Task 2

Now read the following paragraph written about the same topic: the different personalities of two brothers. Again indicate the three parts of the paragraph (*introduction, discussion,* and *conclusion*) with parentheses. Afterwards, fill in the outline below.

> Because my brother and I have very different personalities and interests, many people do not believe that we are brothers or even friends. My brother, Jim, is much friendlier than I am; and he does not like school, whereas I do. In spite of our differences Jim and I are close friends, and our differences only make our relationship as brothers more interesting.

I. (Topic Sentence) ——————————————
   _____
   _____

II. (Discussion)

   A. _____
   _____

   B. _____
   _____

   C. _____
   _____

III. (Conclusion) —————————————————
   _____
   _____

Questions: What is wrong with the proportion?

Which part is the longest?

How does the organization affect the power of the paragraph?

The problem with this paragraph is the *discussion.* The topic sentence tells the reader that the paragraph is about the differences between two brothers, but the discussion only gives two differences without much elaboration. The discussion part of the paragraph is shorter than both the topic sentence and the conclusion.

Choosing the Topic and Writing the Topic Sentence

Before you begin to write a paragraph, you must choose a topic and formulate a complete thought concerning the topic. Your idea will be expressed in your topic sentence. It is necessary to limit your paragraph to one main idea. Then you develop a discussion to illustrate your idea. Finally, your conclusion summarizes the main idea of the paragraph.

A paragraph can be compared to a photograph. In a photograph, attention is usually focused on a dominating subject, and the photographer uses angle, lighting, and composition to say something about the subject. A writer also focuses on a topic in a paragraph and uses words to convey ideas about the topic.

Study the photograph below:

American girl in Florence, Italy, by Ruth Orkin.

What does the photographer consider most important in the photograph?

How does the photographer indicate that the girl walking on the sidewalk is the central focus of the shot?

What is the photographer saying about the girl?

How does the photographer support her idea or perception of the girl?

If you were writing a descriptive paragraph about the photograph, what would your topic sentence be?

POSSIBLE TOPIC SENTENCES:

As the girl walked down the sidewalk, she did her best to ignore the teasing comments and glances from the men relaxing outside.

When the girl returned from her classes, she found herself on a sidewalk among many men who delighted in giving her a hard time.

Writing Task 1

The three paragraphs below are fully developed except for introductory topic sentences. Choose the topic sentence that is implied by the discussion in the paragraph. Circle the letter a, b, or c.

1. _____ (Topic Sentence) _____

At eighty years old she continues to live in her own house and take care of herself. Every week my grandmother sees friends at her regular card games and at church functions. She has always been youthfully active, but she really asserted her youthful self-image two years ago when she began seeing Mr. Thompson, a widower. She now calls him her "boyfriend." I just hope I can be as young as she at eighty.

   a. My grandmother is proud of her good health and quick mind.

   b. My grandmother has refused to become inactive and grow old.

   c. My grandmother lives too far away for me to visit her often.

2. _____ (Topic Sentence) _____

The first indication of this was the lack of clocks in the casinos. Once I asked a card dealer for the time, and he responded, "It's fun time!" Then I realized there were no windows except for a few in the front of the building; I could not even look at the sky for a clue. The absence of time evidently helps business in the casinos.

   a. The casinos in Las Vegas, Nevada, are always crowded until dawn.

  b. Gambling in Las Vegas, Nevada, was one of my most memorable experiences.

  c. When I visited the casinos in Las Vegas, Nevada, I became aware of a plot to forget time.

3. _____ (Topic Sentence)

They have asked us to return old newspapers, bottles, and cans. Other suggestions for decreasing consumption have been to lower the heat in our homes and to avoid unnecessary use of electrical appliances. Because of the environmentalists' efforts many people are more aware now of the need to conserve our resources.

  a. Environmentalists have published their concerns in the leading newspapers.

  b. Environmentalists have asked the public to cut down on its use of the country's natural resources.

  c. Environmentalists have asked politicians to recognize the serious problem of nuclear energy in the U.S.

Writing Task 2

The next three paragraphs are also complete except for introductory topic sentences. Read each paragraph and write a topic sentence on the lines provided. Remember that the topic sentence must relate to the details developed in the discussion.

1. _____

_____

_____

He has been studying the cello since he was seven years old. At first, Keith took lessons from a music teacher in his neighborhood, but his rapid progress made his parents decide to send him to the best cellist in the city. Now, at seventeen, he is concentrating totally on his cello in an effort to get the scholarship that would mean a career in music.

2. _____

_____

_____

Both coastlines are irregular and rocky, but the Oregon coast is dotted with cliffs, whereas the Maine coast is flatter. Pine trees grow along both coasts, and the coastlines have a rugged character because of the trees and rocks. The water in Maine and Oregon is not very warm even in the middle of summer. Perhaps that is why both coasts are not crowded by a lot of tourist spots. The similarities and the differences make the coasts of Maine and Oregon attractive to nature lovers.

3. _____

_____

_____

This romantic idea of the Wild West is portrayed in the many western films the U.S. has produced. Little children grow up playing "cowboys and Indians" because of the influence of movies and television. Even adults are attracted by the West; western clothes and cowboy boots are worn far away from real cowboy country. Both young and old are touched by the magic of the old Wild West.

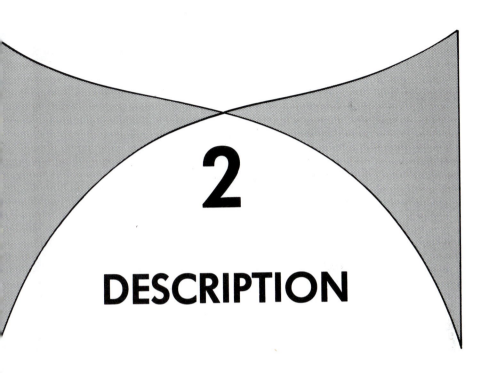

2

DESCRIPTION

PREWRITING STRATEGIES

- When you want to relax after school or work before going home, where do you go?

- Why do you go there? Is it the food, the atmosphere, or the people?

- Describe the place in detail (location, size, objects inside, atmosphere).

Useful vocabulary for discussion:

location

to be located (at, on, near . . .)

size

huge, enormous
tiny
spacious
crowded, cramped

atmosphere

formal, stuffy
informal, casual
cozy
lively
cheerful

Reading Selection

Here is a paragraph describing a favorite place.

On the corner of the street is an old-fashioned° ice-cream shop where people sit on stools° at the counter and eat big ice-cream sundaes°. The counter is very high and made out of beautiful shiny gray marble°. Plates of cake covered with glass rest on top beside jars of candy. In front of the counter are tall wooden stools in a row°. The large containers of many kinds of ice cream are stored° behind the counter along with coffee and tea. On the wall in back of the counter are a large mirror and wooden shelves. Rows of ice-cream glasses are lined up along the shelves. There are also large glass jars filled with a variety of brightly colored candy. The mirror reflects° the candy jars and glasses and adds to the cheerful atmosphere of the shop.

Margin glosses:
from earlier times
seats
dish of ice cream with topping / hard, cold stone
lined up
kept
reproduces

Comprehension

After reading the paragraph, draw the following objects in the correct place in the box.

counter
stools
shelves
cake plate
jars of candy
mirror

WRITING EXERCISES

Organization: Spatial Order

Exercise 1

Study the Reading Selection. Locate the three parts of the paragraph and fill in the outline below.

I. (Topic Sentence) _____

_____

_____

II. (Discussion)

    A. _____

_____

    B. _____

_____

    C. _____

_____

III. (Conclusion) _____

_____

_____

The Reading Selection is organized according to *spatial order* that is based on an order of *physical space.* The following list gives examples of words that can structure a paragraph organized spatially. *Descriptive paragraphs* are often structured by spatial order.

on, at, in
where
under, beneath
over, on top of
at the top of
inside, outside
beside, next to, near
in back (of), in front (of), in the middle (of)

Copyright © 1983 by Harcourt Brace Jovanovich, Inc. All rights reserved.

in between
(to, on) the left, (to, on) the right
(on, in) the corner
across
through
along
beyond
to face
opposite
north, south, east, west (northern, etc.)

Exercise 2

Here is the Reading Selection again. Study it and underline all the
words and phrases that indicate spatial order.

On the corner of the street is an old-fashioned ice-
cream shop where people sit on stools at the counter and
eat big ice-cream sundaes. The counter is very high and
made out of beautiful shiny gray marble. Plates of cake
covered with glass rest on top beside jars of candy. In front
of the counter are tall wooden stools in a row. The large
containers of many kinds of ice cream are stored behind
the counter along with coffee and tea. On the wall in back
of the counter are a large mirror and wooden shelves.
Rows of ice-cream glasses are lined up along the shelves.
There are also large glass jars filled with a variety of
brightly colored candy. The mirror reflects the candy jars
and glasses and adds to the cheerful atmosphere of the
shop.

Exercise 3

Study the diagram below of *a room in the library.* Write five sentences describing where the objects are in the room. Use spatial vocabulary.

Copyright © 1983 by Harcourt Brace Jovanovich, Inc. All rights reserved.

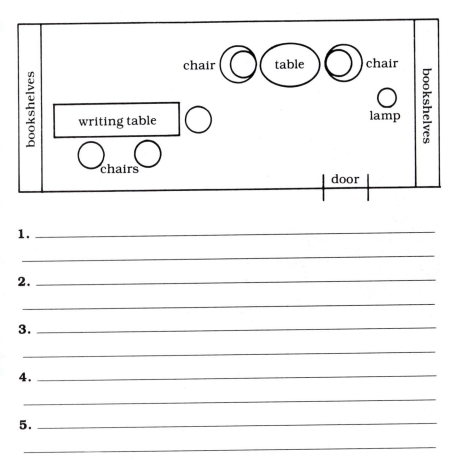

1. _____

   _____

2. _____

   _____

3. _____

   _____

4. _____

   _____

5. _____

   _____

Exercise 4

MODEL PARAGRAPH: Study the following descriptive paragraph.
Underline the topic sentence. Circle all words and phrases that signal spatial order.

My college is located in the middle of a residential
neighborhood in a big city. Inside the front gate is a truck
selling coffee and refreshments to passing students and
teachers. To the left of the truck is the administration
building where many of the offices are located. There is
usually a large crowd of students standing and talking to

Copyright © 1983 by Harcourt Brace Jovanovich, Inc. All rights reserved.

their friends in front of this building. Opposite the administration building is an old classroom building, and in between these two buildings is a large, attractive square with grass and trees. Across from the front gate on the far side of the square is a tall building with a large clock on top. As you walk through the campus, there are four or five newer classroom buildings; one faces the library. At the southern end of the campus is another gate, and beyond the gate are two bookstores and a variety of food and clothing shops.

Exercise 5

Write a descriptive paragraph about a favorite place; for example, your room, a restaurant, a store, or the place you like to go after school or work. Fill in the outline below with your topic sentence,

Copyright © 1983 by Harcourt Brace Jovanovich, Inc. All rights reserved.

some details to be used in your discussion, and your concluding sentence. Use some spatial vocabulary to structure your paragraph. Study the list of examples and the sample paragraph above before writing. Write your paragraph on notebook paper.

I.   (Topic Sentence) _____

_____

_____

II. (Discussion)

    A. _____

_____

    B. _____

_____

    C. _____

_____

III. (Conclusion) _____

_____

_____

Development: Topic Sentences

The following two paragraphs are complete except for introductory topic sentences. Read each paragraph and write a *topic sentence that relates to the details developed in the discussion.*

1. _____

_____

He smiles and jokes with anyone who comes into the store to buy a morning paper. His big smile displays beautiful white teeth, and his bushy beard and curly hair make him look even more cheerful. When he laughs, his large stomach shakes and jiggles. His friendly and warm personality cheers up the day for everyone who meets him.

Copyright © 1983 by Harcourt Brace Jovanovich, Inc. All rights reserved.

2. _____

_____

Whenever he has coffee, he insists on drinking it from that particular mug. It is white and has a picture of a black horse on one side.
The shape is perfectly cylindrical, and the handle is simple and
sturdy. There is a small crack that runs down one side of the cup,
but John does not care. Even in bad condition the mug will always
be his favorite because it was his grandfather's.

Sentence Combining

Combine each group of sentences to make one sentence and write it
on the lines below. The sentences will then make a descriptive
paragraph about a mystery object. Try to guess what the object is.
The vocabulary cues at the right will help you combine the
sentences.

Example: **a.** Bill felt hungry.
             b. Bill had no lunch today.   (because)

             *Bill felt hungry because he had no lunch
             today.*

1.   **a.** The object looks long.
      b. The object looks thin.   (and)
      c. The object measures about 8 inches in length.

2.   **a.** The object has many flat sides.
      b. The object appears rounded.   (but)
      c. The object has a diameter.   (with)
      d. The diameter measures about 1/8 inch.   (of or that)

3.   **a.** It comes in many colors outside.   (and)
      b. It comes in many colors inside.   (but)
      c. Usually the outside is yellow.   (and or while)
      d. Usually the inside is grayish black.

4.   **a.** There is often writing along the outside of the   (and)
      object.

Copyright © 1983 by Harcourt Brace Jovanovich, Inc. All rights reserved.

    b. There is often a number along the outside of   (which or such as)
       the object.
    c. The number is often a 2 or a 3.

5.   **a.** The top of the object is made of rubber.   (with)
    b. The top of the object has an aluminum band   (and)
       around it.
    c. The bottom of the object comes to a sharp
       point.

6.   **a.** The body of the object appears to be made of
       wood.   (but or while)
    b. The inside of the object is actually made of
       lead.

7.   **a.** The longer you use the object, the shorter it
       gets.   (and)
    b. The longer you use the object, the duller it
       gets.

8.   **a.** The object is often used by students.
    b. The object is often used by artists.   (and)
    c. The object is often used by office workers.

_____

_____

_____

_____

_____

_____

_____

_____

_____

_____

_____

_____

Copyright © 1983 by Harcourt Brace Jovanovich, Inc. All rights reserved.

Proofreading

The following version of the Reading Selection contains ten mistakes. The errors are faulty subject-verb agreement (3), prepositions (2), run-on sentences (1), articles (3), and fragments (1). Find the mistakes and correct them.

Example: One of the friends are going.

            One of the friends is going.

1   On the corner of the street is an old-fashioned ice-cream

2   shop that people sit in stools at the counter and eats big

3   ice-cream sundaes. The counter is very high and made out of

4   beautiful, shiny, gray marble, plates of cake covered with glass

5   rest on top beside jars of candy. In front of the counter are tall

6   wooden stools in a row. The larger containers of many kinds of

7   ice cream is stored behind the counter along with coffee and tea.

8   On the wall at back of a counter are a large mirror and wooden

9   shelves. Rows of ice-cream glasses are lined up along the shelves.

10   There are also large glass jars filled with the variety of brightly

11   colored candy. The mirror reflects the candy jars and glasses.

12   Adds to the cheerful atmosphere of the shop.

Copyright © 1983 by Harcourt Brace Jovanovich, Inc. All rights reserved.

FORMAL WRITING

Writing Topics

Choose one of the three topics below and write a descriptive paragraph. Remember to state your topic sentence in the *introduction*, to develop your *discussion* completely, and to summarize or restate your topic sentence in the *conclusion*. Try to use spatial and descriptive vocabulary. If you find it helpful, outline the three parts of the paragraph before writing. Write your paragraph on notebook composition paper.

1. Describe a place.

2. Describe a person. (You will not need as much spatial vocabulary for this topic.)

3. Describe an object.

After you write your paragraph, use the checklist below to help you edit your paragraph. Make sure you have done everything on the list.

Checklist

ORGANIZATION

1. Is your topic sentence in the introduction?
2. Does the discussion develop and support your topic sentence?
3. Does your conclusion summarize or restate your topic sentence?

GRAMMAR
Have you checked for errors in the following?

1. verb tense sequence
2. subject-verb agreement
3. pronoun agreement
4. articles
5. prepositions
6. sentence boundaries (run-ons and fragments)

VOCABULARY

1. Have you used spatial and descriptive vocabulary to structure your paragraph?
2. Have you checked difficult words for correct spelling?

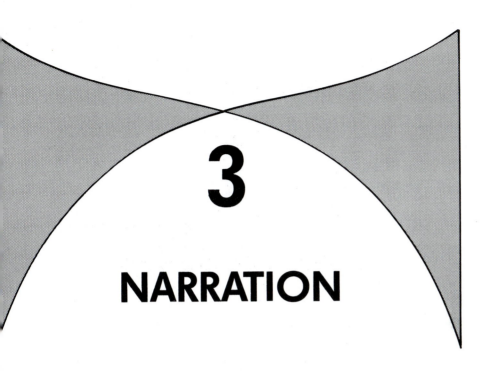

3

NARRATION

PREWRITING STRATEGIES

- Do you ever reminisce about your childhood?

- Does nostalgia affect your memories of childhood? Can you remember things as they actually were?

- If you could go back in time, would you want to relive a certain period in your childhood? Which would it be?

- Can you remember something in your childhood that made you feel very happy, sad, afraid, or angry? Describe what happened and why it made you feel this way.

Useful vocabulary for discussion:

to remember
to remind . . . of
to reminisce about
to be nostalgic about
to relive
to grow up
to become an adult
nostalgia
childhood
adulthood
memory
memorable

Reading Selection

Here is a narrative paragraph describing a childhood memory of a language classroom.

My second-grade French teacher ruined° my first experience learning a new language. At first we were only expected to master° simple phrases such as "hello," "how are you?" and "what is your name?" But soon after we had to memorize° poems and songs. This may sound like fun and games, but our teacher was like a drill sergeant°. As the term went on, her expectations grew more and more unreasonable°. Each afternoon she lined us up at the top of the staircase to say "au revoir°." The three-o'clock bell rang, and we still stood there. We had to perfect our accents and strain° our little voices to please her. One of us usually burst into tears° out of fear or frustration° at her criticisms. Because of these horrible experiences, I forgot most of my early French. However, I will never forgive° or forget my second-grade teacher.

(marginal glosses:)
destroyed
learn

learn by heart

military trainer
ridiculous, unfair
goodbye (French)
force, try hard
began to cry
discouragement

excuse

Discussion Questions

1. At what age did you begin to study a foreign language?

2. What was the atmosphere like in the learning situation?

3. How did you react to studying a new language?

4. Do you agree with the experts who say that it is better to study a foreign language as a young child? Why or why not?

WRITING EXERCISES

Organization: Chronological Order

Exercise 1

Study the Reading Selection. Locate the three parts of the paragraph and fill in the outline below.

I. (Topic Sentence) _____

_____

_____

II. (Discussion)

    A. _____

_____

    B. _____

_____

    C. _____

_____

III. (Conclusion) _____

_____

_____

The Reading Selection is organized according to chronological order. *Chronological order* is based on a *time sequence.* The following list gives examples of words that can structure a paragraph organized chronologically. *Narrative* paragraphs, or paragraphs that tell a story, are often structured by chronological order to tell the reader what happened first, second, third, and so on.

always, usually, often, sometimes, seldom, rarely, never
in the beginning, at first, at the start
now, nowadays
when
before, after
once
while, during

Copyright © 1983 by Harcourt Brace Jovanovich, Inc. All rights reserved.

next, then, soon
since
earlier, later
first, second, third, etc.
at (the hour), on (the day), in (the month, season, year)
at birth, in childhood, in adolescence, as an adult
in the morning/afternoon/evening, at night
eventually
at last, in conclusion, finally

Exercise 2

Here is the Reading Selection again. Study it and underline all words
and phrases that indicate chronological order.

My second-grade French teacher ruined my first experience learning a new language. At first we were only
expected to master simple phrases such as "hello," "how
are you?" and "what is your name?" But soon after we had
to memorize poems and songs. This may sound like fun
and games, but our teacher was like a drill sergeant. As
the term went on, her expectations grew more and more
unreasonable. Each afternoon she lined us up at the top of
the staircase to say "au revoir." The three-o'clock bell rang,
and we still stood there. We had to perfect our accents and
strain our little voices to please her. One of us usually
burst into tears out of fear or frustration at her criticisms.
Because of these horrible experiences, I forgot most of my
early French. However, I will never forgive or forget my
second-grade teacher.

Exercise 3

Each group of sentences below makes up a paragraph, but the sentences are not listed in correct chronological order. Study them and
underline all chronological vocabulary. Then arrange them in correct order by putting the number 1, 2, or 3 before the sentence.

Copyright © 1983 by Harcourt Brace Jovanovich, Inc. All rights reserved.

1. _____ After finishing my morning chores, I get my books and drive to school.
   _____ During class I drink a second cup of coffee to perk me up.
   _____ At the start of each day I make breakfast, get dressed, and walk the dog.
   _____ My first class begins at nine o'clock.
   _____ I always lie in bed planning my day before I get up in the morning.

2. _____ But once he got started, the room's appearance improved quickly.
   _____ When his mother walked by, she could not believe how neat it was.
   _____ Jeff decided to clean his room last weekend.
   _____ After three hours of hard work he could hardly recognize it.
   _____ The job looked overwhelming at first.

Exercise 4

MODEL PARAGRAPH: Study the following narrative paragraph structured by a time sequence. Underline the topic sentence. Circle all words and phrases that signal chronological order.

Last Saturday good friends from college visited, and I wanted to give them an exciting tour of my new home. First, I took them to my favorite café in the Italian section of the city. After coffee and pastries we went to the science museum because it was having an exhibition of photographs of Saturn. It was difficult tearing my friends away from the exhibit, but at six o'clock we began to think about supper. We finally agreed on a Japanese restaurant near the museum for an early dinner. To top off the day we saw a popular play. By the end of the evening we were all ready for rest and quiet.

Copyright © 1983 by Harcourt Brace Jovanovich, Inc. All rights reserved.

Exercise 5

Write a paragraph about what you did last Saturday, or on your last vacation, or on your last birthday. Fill in the outline below with your topic sentence, some details to be used in your discussion, and your concluding sentence. Remember to use some chronological vocabulary to structure your paragraph. Study the list of examples and the model paragraph above before writing. Write your paragraph on notebook paper.

I. (Topic Sentence) _____

_____

_____

II. (Discussion)

A. _____

_____

B. _____

_____

C. _____

_____

III. (Conclusion) _____

_____

_____

Development: Completeness of the Paragraph

In our discussion in the first chapter we said that all the sentences in the paragraph relate to the topic sentence. In a complete paragraph the topic sentence is fully explained and supported by the discussion. When the topic sentence is not supported or explained, the reader gets confused and loses patience with the writer. Because the writer has written an incomplete paragraph, he has made communication difficult.

The narrative paragraph below is structured by a time sequence, but it is not complete because some information is missing. You must complete the time sequence. Write the paragraph again as you insert the sentences necessary to fill in the time sequence.

Copyright © 1983 by Harcourt Brace Jovanovich, Inc. All rights reserved.

After graduating from art school Marcia began to look for a job with an advertising agency in Boston. She set up interviews at three different companies on the first day. During the first interview she was quite nervous, but she began to relax during the second interview. Sitting on the bus on the way back to her apartment, Marcia found it hard to believe that she had found a job at last.

_____

_____

_____

_____

_____

_____

_____

_____

_____

_____

_____

_____

Sentence Combining

Combine each group of sentences to make one sentence and write it on the lines below. The sentences will then make a narrative paragraph. The vocabulary cues at the right will help you combine the sentences.

Example: **a.** Katherine woke up.   (when)
             b. The alarm clock rang loudly at
                 7:00 A.M.

When the alarm clock rang loudly at
7:00 A.M., Katherine woke up.

Copyright © 1983 by Harcourt Brace Jovanovich, Inc. All rights reserved.

1. **a.** David and Peter went on a camping trip.
    b. They went to the White Mountains in New Hampshire.
    c. They went in June.

2. **a.** They checked all their equipment.   (after or before)
    b. They got into the car for the long ride to the mountains.

3. **a.** They arrived at the campground in the late   (when or after)
    afternoon.
    b. They set up camp near a small stream.

4. **a.** David put up the tent.   (while)
    b. Peter cooked supper over the fire.

5. **a.** They crawled into their sleeping bags at   (when or after)
    sunset.
    b. They became nervous.   (because)
    c. They began to hear animal noises.

6. **a.** Peter wanted to get up and go to the car.   (but)
    b. David said it would be better just to go to sleep.

7. **a.** They got up at sunrise.   (and)
    b. They got up before the other campers.
    c. They made a hearty breakfast.

8. **a.** David and Peter prepared for a long hike.   (and)
    b. It was their first hike.
    c. They decided to go to the top of Mount Madison.

9. **a.** They began the climb.   (when or as)
    b. It started to rain.   (and or so)
    c. They decided to go home.

_____

_____

_____

_____

_____

Copyright © 1983 by Harcourt Brace Jovanovich, Inc. All rights reserved.

_____

_____

_____

_____

_____

_____

_____

_____

_____

_____

_____

_____

Proofreading

The following version of the Reading Selection contains ten mistakes. The errors are faulty subject-verb agreement (1), pronoun agreement (3), articles (1), prepositions (1), verb tense (2), run-on sentences (1), and fragments (1). Find the mistakes and correct them.

1   My second-grade French teacher ruined my first experience

2 learning a new language. At first we was only expected to master

3 simple phrases such as "hello," "how are you?" and "what is your

4 name?" But soon after they had to memorize poems and songs.

5 This may sound like fun and games, but our teacher is like a drill

6 sergeant. As term went on her expectations grew more and more

7 unreasonable, each afternoon she lined us up in the top of the

8 staircase to say "au revoir." The three-o'clock bell rang, and we

Copyright © 1983 by Harcourt Brace Jovanovich, Inc. All rights reserved.

9 still stand there. We had to perfect your accents and strain our

10 little voices to please her. One of us usually burst into tears out

11 of fear or frustration at his criticisms. Because of these horrible

12 experiences. I forgot most of my early French. However, I will

13 never forgive or forget my second-grade teacher.

Copyright © 1983 by Harcourt Brace Jovanovich, Inc. All rights reserved.

FORMAL WRITING

Writing Topics

Choose one of the three topics below or one of your own and write a narrative paragraph about the topic. Remember to state your topic sentence in the *introduction*, to develop your *discussion* completely, and to summarize or restate your topic sentence in the *conclusion*. Try to use the chronological vocabulary you have been practicing in this chapter. If you find it helpful, outline the three parts of the paragraph before writing. Write your paragraph on notebook composition paper.

1. a childhood memory

2. a memorable trip or holiday

3. your first day at a new school or new job

After you write your paragraph, use the checklist below to help you edit your paragraph. Make sure you have done everything on the list.

Checklist

ORGANIZATION

1. Is your topic sentence in the introduction?
2. Does the discussion develop and support your topic sentence?
3. Does your conclusion summarize or restate the topic sentence?

GRAMMAR
Have you checked for errors in the following?

1. verb tense sequence
2. subject-verb agreement
3. pronoun agreement
4. articles
5. prepositions
6. sentence boundaries

VOCABULARY

1. Have you used chronological vocabulary to structure your paragraph?
2. Have you checked difficult words for correct spelling?

4

GENERALIZATIONS AND SPECIFICS

PREWRITING STRATEGIES

- Do you remember your dreams?
- Do you ever dream the same dream again and again? If so, describe it.
- When you were a child, did you have nightmares? What were they about?
- How often do you think you dream?
- Do you ever dream in English?
- Why do people dream?

Useful vocabulary for discussion:

to dream of/about
to have a dream
to have a nightmare
to daydream
to fantasize
fantasy
dreamer
to interpret
interpretation
to analyze
analysis
to symbolize
symbol
symbolic

Dream for Interpretation

In small groups, study the following dream narrative and interpret
its meaning. The underlined words are symbolic and should help
you in your analysis.

On the night before his college entrance examina-
tions, a young student had the following dream:

As I walked slowly down the street toward the <u>train
station</u>, I suddenly heard the <u>train whistle</u> blow. I began to
run to catch the <u>train</u>, but when I finally reached the plat-
form, <u>the doors closed</u> in my face. I stood still trying to
catch my breath while the <u>train left without me</u>.

Reading Selection

Here is a paragraph describing the role of dreams in a particular
culture.

Because dreaming is considered a very important part of life,
the people of the Senoi tribe° of Malaysia generally try to control
the events in a dream and make the dream end in a positive way.
One of the Senoi guidelines° to control dreams is "face and defeat°
danger." For instance, if a child dreams that a large, frightening

social group

rules / beat,
conquer

animal is chasing him, the child should not run away or try to wake up. Instead he is encouraged° to turn around and face the animal. If the animal attacks° him, then the child should fight back. Even being wounded° or killed in a dream is a good experi- ence because the dreamer has lessened° the strength of the ani- mal during the fight. This example shows how the dreamer can create a positive end to a dream by being in control.

advised	
tries to hurt	
hurt	
decreased	

Discussion Questions

1. When you have a nightmare, do you try to interpret it or forget it?

2. Do you share your dreams and nightmares with other people? Who do you tell them to?

3. In the Senoi tribe the dreamer is supposed to confront danger in a dream. Do you think it is possible to control your actions in a dream. How?

4. What are the advantages to controlling dreams?

WRITING EXERCISES

Organization: Generalizations and Specifics

The Reading Selection begins with a *generalization* that is illustrated by a *specific example*. A *generalization* is a statement about something that is widely accepted most of the time.

For example:

A university education prepares a person for a career.

Interesting hobbies make a person's life fuller.

Travel before the automobile was limited.

In the U.S. life in the city is more dangerous than in small towns.

Specific details support or prove the generalization by giving facts, examples, and personal experiences.

For example: Here are three details which support the generalization that "In the U.S. life in the city is more dangerous than in small towns."

1. Because of overpopulation there is more crime in the city.

2. Industry causes a high degree of air pollution.

3. Crowded traffic conditions create more accidents.

The following list gives some vocabulary you can use when you state a *generalization.*

in general
generally
on the whole
in most cases
as a rule
all, every
always, usually, frequently, often, sometimes, rarely, seldom, never

Here are some words used when supporting a generalization with *specific details.*

Copyright © 1983 by Harcourt Brace Jovanovich, Inc. All rights reserved.

for example
for instance
for one thing
in other words
let me illustrate
to illustrate
to prove
as an illustration
as an example
as proof

Exercise 1

Here is the Reading Selection again. Study it and underline any words and phrases that indicate *generalizations* or *specific details*.

Because dreaming is considered a very important part of life, the people of the Senoi tribe of Malaysia generally try to control the events in a dream and make the dream end in a positive way. One of the Senoi guidelines to control dreams is "face and defeat danger." For instance, if a child dreams that a large, frightening animal is chasing him, the child should not run away or try to wake up. Instead he is encouraged to turn around and face the animal. If the animal attacks him, then the child should fight back. Even being wounded or killed in a dream is a good experience because the dreamer has lessened the strength of the animal during the fight. This example shows how the dreamer can create a positive end to a dream by being in control.

Exercise 2

After reading each group of specific details (a, b, c), write a logical generalization.

Copyright © 1983 by Harcourt Brace Jovanovich, Inc. All rights reserved.

1. _____

_____

_____

   a. In the early 1900s many Americans were forced to work six or seven days a week to earn a living.

   b. By 1950 most Americans worked only five days a week with daily lunch and coffee breaks.

   c. In the 1980s some Americans are demanding three- and four-day work weeks.

2. _____

_____

_____

   a. A newborn baby can distinguish color from black and white.

   b. If you move an object before her face, her eyes and head will follow it.

   c. A new baby's eyes will focus on an object held close to her face.

3. _____

_____

_____

   a. Smoking cigarettes brings tar and nicotine into the lungs.

   b. Smoking causes shortness of breath.

   c. Smoking makes the heart work harder.

Exercise 3

MODEL PARAGRAPH: Study the following paragraph. Underline the generalization and circle all words and phrases that indicate generalization or specific details.

On the whole my roommate, Bill, is one of the slop-
piest people I know. For one thing he leaves his dirty

Copyright © 1983 by Harcourt Brace Jovanovich, Inc. All rights reserved.

clothes all over his room. Another example of his sloppy behavior is the mess he always makes at dinner. He drops crumbs on the kitchen table, chairs, and the floor, as well as gets food stains on his shirt and tie. People say that he is just as bad at work. In other words there are papers all over his desk, half-empty cups of coffee and cans of soda, old cigarette stubs, and papers all over the floor. As a rule Bill leaves a trail of garbage wherever he goes.

Exercise 4

Write a paragraph stating a generalization and support it with specific details. Choose either:

My friend is a very _____ person.
or
My (brother, sister, father, mother) is a very _____ person.

Fill in the outline with your generalization, some specific details to be used in the discussion, and your conclusion. Remember to use some of the structure vocabulary for generalizations and specific details. Study the vocabulary list and the above model paragraph before writing. Write your paragraph on notebook composition paper.

I.   (Topic Sentence) _____

_____

_____

II.   (Discussion)

    A. _____

_____

    B. _____

_____

    C. _____

_____

Copyright © 1983 by Harcourt Brace Jovanovich, Inc. All rights reserved.

III. (Conclusion) ————————————————————

————————————————————————

————————————————————————

Development: Unity of the Paragraph

Unity refers to the connection every sentence in the paragraph has to the main idea in the topic sentence. That is, every sentence in the paragraph must relate directly to the topic sentence. The diagram below illustrates how the topic sentence is the central focus in the unified paragraph with the supporting sentences all connected to it. Anything in the paragraph that does not relate to the topic sentence is irrelevant information; it does not belong and should be left out.

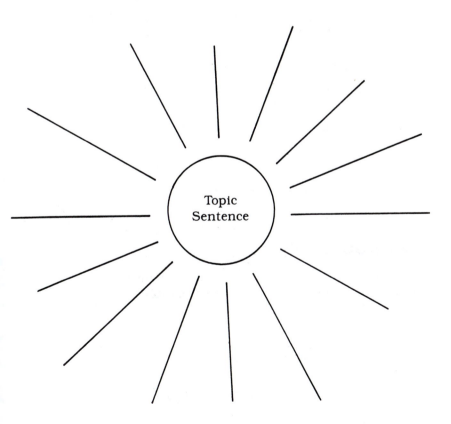

Topic
Sentence

Copyright © 1983 by Harcourt Brace Jovanovich, Inc. All rights reserved.

Read the generalization and find the specific detail that does not support the generalization. Put an X in front of it. Three of the details support the generalization.

1. Generalization: Starting your own business requires many skills and resources.

   Specific Details:

   _____ **a.** You need enough money to cover the initial costs.

   _____ **b.** You can be your own boss if you own a business.

   _____ **c.** Personal contacts in business are always helpful for advice and discounts.

   _____ **d.** Recordkeeping and management ability are essential.

2. Generalization: In India a large family is often considered financially beneficial, and in general children are regarded as a form of wealth.

   Specific Details:

   _____ **a.** At an early age children help around the home and business.

   _____ **b.** Children work and bring in money when they are older.

   _____ **c.** Boys are more desirable than girls.

   _____ **d.** When the parents are old, the children take care of them.

Sentence Combining

Combine each group of sentences to make one sentence and write the sentences on the lines below in paragraph form. Use the cues at the right to combine the sentences.

Example: **a.** I will go to the party.   (if)
            b. I finish my work.

            I will go to the party if I finish my work.

Copyright © 1983 by Harcourt Brace Jovanovich, Inc. All rights reserved.

1.   **a.** I have never understood a certain proverb.   (that or which)
      b. The proverb says, "You cannot have your cake and eat it, too."

2.   **a.** My mother once interpreted it for me.   (and)
      b. She told me that it meant you cannot have everything.

3.   **a.** For example, it is impossible to find a job that pays well.   (and)
      b. It is impossible to find a job that interests you all the time.
      c. It is impossible to find a job that challenges you every day.

4.   **a.** That may be true.   (but, yet, or however)
      b. I have often wondered why it has to be that way.

5.   **a.** Why is it impossible to have everything?   (and or or)
      b. Why is it impossible to be completely satisified?

6.   **a.** You think about the illustration of the cake.   (if or when)
      b. It does not make sense.

7.   **a.** Who would make a cake?   (and or but)
      b. Who would not enjoy eating it afterwards?

8.   **a.** There is definitely something wrong with the logic of the illustration.   (if or when)
      b. You consider it carefully.

_____

_____

_____

_____

_____

_____

_____

_____

Copyright © 1983 by Harcourt Brace Jovanovich, Inc. All rights reserved.

_____

_____

_____

_____

_____

_____

_____

Proofreading

The following version of the Reading Selection contains nine mistakes. The errors are faulty subject-verb agreement (4), pronoun agreement (1), articles (2), plurality (1), and demonstrative adjectives (1). Find the mistakes and correct them.

1   Because dreaming is considered the very important part of

2 life, the people of the Senoi tribe of Malaysia generally tries to

3 control the events in a dream and makes the dream end in a

4 positive way. One of the Senoi guideline to control dreams is

5 "face and defeat danger." For instance, if a child dreams that a

6 large, frightening animal is chasing you, the child should not

7 run away or try to wake up. Instead he is encouraged to turn

8 around and face an animal. If the animal attack him, then the

9 child should fight back. Even being wounded or killed in a

10 dream are a good experience because the dreamer has lessened

11 the strength of the animal during the fight. That example shows

12 how the dreamer can create a positive end to a dream by being in

13 control.

Copyright © 1983 by Harcourt Brace Jovanovich, Inc. All rights reserved.

FORMAL WRITING

Writing Topics

Choose one of the three topics below or one of your own and write a paragraph supporting a generalization with specific details. Try to use the structure vocabulary you have been practicing in the chapter. Outline the three parts of the paragraph before writing if you find it helpful. Write your paragraph on notebook paper.

1.   Illustrate a generalization about (your) life with an anecdote or short story.

2.   Illustrate a proverb with an example or personal experience.

3.   Illustrate a generalization about the U.S. or your native country with facts, examples, and personal experiences.

After you write your paragraph, use the checklist below to help you edit your work. Make sure you have done everything on the list.

Checklist

ORGANIZATION

1.   Is your topic sentence in the introduction? Does it express your generalization?
2.   Does the discussion develop and support your topic sentence with specific details?
3.   Does your conclusion summarize or restate your topic sentence?

GRAMMAR
Have you checked for errors in the following?

1.   verb tense sequence
2.   subject-verb agreement
3.   pronoun agreement
4.   articles
5.   prepositions
6.   sentence boundaries

VOCABULARY

1.   Have you used the structure vocabulary in the chapter to introduce generalizations and specific details?
2.   Have you checked difficult words for correct spelling?

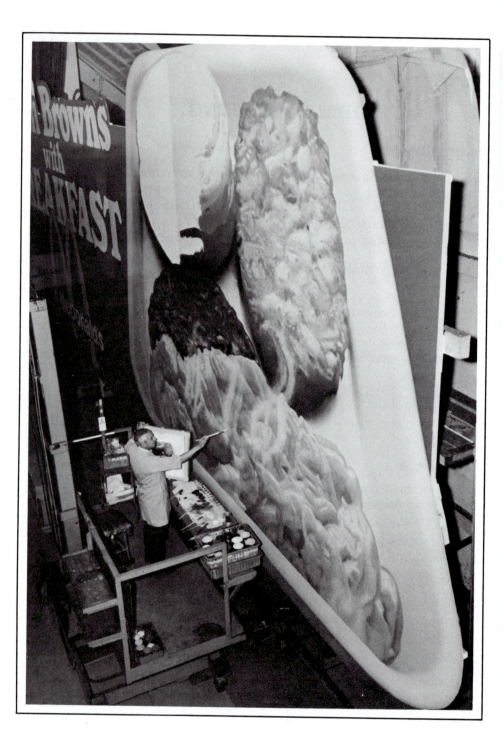

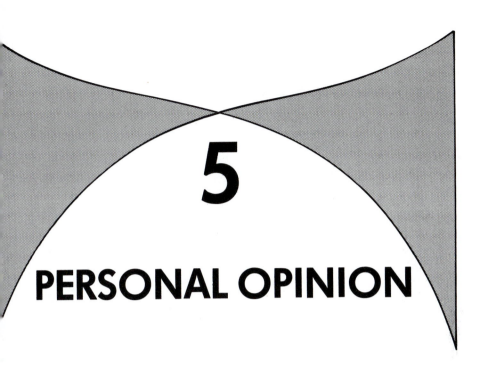

5

PERSONAL OPINION

PREWRITING STRATEGIES

- How much are you influenced by advertisements when buying a product?

- Is it possible to ignore advertisements? Explain your answer.

- Which advertisements are most effective: magazine and newspaper ads, television and radio commercials, billboards, or subway posters?

- What are some of your favorite TV commercials? Why do you like them so much?

- Would you like to read a magazine that has no advertisements? Why or why not?

- Should you believe everything an advertisement claims? Why or why not?

Useful vocabulary for discussion:

to advertise
an advertiser
an advertisement, an ad
a manufacturer
a product
merchandise
brand (name)
commercial
billboard
slogan
sales pitch
strategy
to consume
a consumer
to persuade
to influence
to appeal to emotion
to lie
to deceive
to boast
to exaggerate

GROUP ACTIVITY: Students should each bring in two colorful magazine ads: one they like and one they do not like. In small groups students can study the advertisements and answer the following questions:

1. What strategies has the advertiser used to make the product appealing? (use of color, scenery, people, slogans)

2. What kind of people is the ad trying to attract? (people of a certain age, sex, profession, and having particular interests)

3. Is it obvious which product is being advertised?

4. Can you find instances of exaggeration or lying? Give examples.

5. Does the ad give you any new information? What is it?

6. How would you rate the advertisement on a scale of one to ten?

Reading Selection

Here is a personal opinion paragraph about advertising.

> In my opinion advertising is nothing but a money-making plot° to control our lives. Television and radio commercials, as well as newspaper, magazine, and subway ads, all cry out to us "BUY, BUY, BUY." I believe that their catchy° songs and slogans, bright, attractive ads, and beautiful models all conspire° to sell us products we either do not want or do not need. Even when we do need to buy something, we usually buy it for the wrong reason. Colorful packages and amusing ads get better sale results than actual quality does. In addition, many commercials are misleading° or dishonest and give the public false information. It is clear to me that until we stop believing everything we see and hear in advertisements, they will continue to control us.

plan

easily liked and remembered / plan

give the wrong idea

Discussion Questions

1. Do you agree or disagree with the opinion expressed in the reading selection?

2. **a.** If you agree with the writer, can you add any other supportive arguments that were not mentioned in the paragraph?
    b. If you disagree, which specific details do you object to?

3. Discuss some of the advantages of advertising such as it being an information source, creating mass markets, and providing entertainment.

4. How can the government protect the consumer from false advertising?

WRITING EXERCISES

Organization: Personal Opinion

The reading selection expresses a *personal opinion*. The writer's opinion is stated in the topic sentence. The discussion section includes supportive details that relate to the topic sentence. The conclusion restates or summarizes the personal opinion. Below is a list of words and phrases that signal personal opinion.

in my opinion
from my point of view
in my view
it seems to me that
it is clear (to me) that
I think
I believe
I suppose
I agree, I disagree
I am certain, I am sure

Exercise 1

Now study the Reading Selection and underline the words and phrases that indicate personal opinion.

In my opinion advertising is nothing but a money-making plot to control our lives. Television and radio commercials, as well as newspaper, magazine, and subway ads, all cry out to us "BUY, BUY, BUY." I believe that their catchy songs and slogans, bright, attractive ads, and beautiful models all conspire to sell us products we either do not want or do not need. Even when we do need to buy something, we usually buy it for the wrong reason. Colorful packages and amusing ads get better sale results than actual quality does. In addition, many commercials are misleading or dishonest and give the public false information. It is clear to me that until we stop believing every-

Copyright © 1983 by Harcourt Brace Jovanovich, Inc. All rights reserved.

thing we see and hear in advertisements, they will continue to control us.

Exercise 2: Values Clarification

TASK:

a. Study the problem and facts below.
b. Decide on a solution to the problem.
c. Write your opinion in the outline below and give at least three reasons that support your idea in the space for supportive details.

PROBLEM:

Ted and Laura Wallace are a happily married couple who live in New York City. They do not have any plans to have children. Both of them are professionals and have good jobs. Ted has been offered a better job in Atlanta, Georgia, which will lead to career advancement. He wants to take the new, challenging job, but Laura does not want to leave her excellent job in New York. What should they do?

FACTS:

Ted Wallace: happily married for five years
34 years old
lawyer
B.A., J.D. (law degree)
earns $30,000 per year
likes New York
bored with present job
lawyers are needed in many cities
wants to try a new job
the new job pays $35,000 per year
marriage and career are both important to
   him

Laura Wallace: happily married for five years
31 years old
artist for advertising agency
B.A. and M.A. in design and graphic arts
earns $25,000 per year
likes New York
likes her job
does not think she can find a job in her field
   in Atlanta
marriage and career are both important to
   her

Copyright © 1983 by Harcourt Brace Jovanovich, Inc. All rights reserved.

OUTLINE

I.   (Personal Opinion) _____

_____

_____

II.   (Supportive Details)

   A. _____

   _____

   B. _____

   _____

   C. _____

   _____

   D. _____

   _____

Exercise 3

MODEL PARAGRAPH   Study the following personal opinion paragraph. Underline the topic sentence that expresses the opinion. Circle all words and phrases that signal personal opinion.

I am certain that we eat for more reasons than just
providing our bodies with the energy they need to func-
tion. For instance, some people are very particular about
what they eat for nourishment, and food becomes a sen-
sual pleasure for them. Others use food as a means for
creation as they cook elaborate and unusual meals. But
one of the most important reasons for eating, from my
point of view, is the social fulfillment it gives when family
and friends come together to share the events of the day
and ideas as well as the food. It seems to me that these
reasons for eating may be as important as the need for
nourishment.

Copyright © 1983 by Harcourt Brace Jovanovich, Inc. All rights reserved.

Exercise 4: Values Clarification Paragraph

TASK:

a. Read the problem and study the facts.
b. Decide on your opinion. Should Bill go to college or take over his father's business?
c. Write a personal opinion paragraph using some of the personal opinion words and phrases introduced in this chapter. Before writing, fill in the outline with your opinion stated in the topic sentence, some details for your discussion, and a conclusion restating your opinion.

PROBLEM:

Bill Carpenter is a recent high-school graduate. He cannot decide whether to continue his education or work in the family business.

FACTS:

Bill is a good student with a promising future.
He has been offered a scholarship at a well-known university.
As a child, Bill dreamed of becoming a doctor one day.
The job market for college graduates is competitive, and starting salaries are low.
Bill's family has owned and operated a successful restaurant for over fifty years.
Bill's father wants to retire this year and leave Bill the business.
If Bill refuses the restaurant, the family will have to sell it.
The restaurant makes $200,000 a year in profits.

OUTLINE

I.   (Topic Sentence) _____

_____

_____

II. (Supporting Details)

    A. _____

_____

    B. _____

_____

    C. _____

_____

Copyright © 1983 by Harcourt Brace Jovanovich, Inc. All rights reserved.

D. _____

_____

III. (Conclusion) _____

_____

_____

Development: Coherence of the Paragraph

Coherence exists when all the sentences in the paragraph are connected in a smooth, logical order. In other words, each thought is connected to the one before and after. The reader who has to struggle with the incoherent paragraph often gives up feeling frustrated, and the writer's efforts fail to communicate the point.

Two tools the writer may use to connect sentences so that they make sense to the reader are *referents* and *connectives.*

Referents are words that substitute for other words the way pronouns substitute for nouns (book → it). They can either refer back to ideas already mentioned or forward to ideas that have not been expressed yet. Some examples of referents are listed below:

it
this, these, that, those
mine, yours, etc.

Connectives are words that link ideas by defining their relationship to one another. The four basic relationships between ideas are *addition, contrast, time,* and *result.* Below are some examples of each type of connective:

addition: and, in addition, also, furthermore
contrast: but, however, although, nevertheless
time: after, before, next, finally
result: as a result, because, consequently, therefore, if . . . then

TASK:

The paragraph below contains referents and connectives that help to make it coherent.

Copyright © 1983 by Harcourt Brace Jovanovich, Inc. All rights reserved.

a. Circle all referents and connectives.
b. List each referent below and fill in the word or words it refers to in the space provided (the first one has been done for you)
c. List each connective in the space provided and write down the appropriate category it falls under (addition, contrast, time, or result)

1   In my opinion, most Americans are weight conscious.

2 Consequently, they are very concerned with the size and shape of

3 their bodies. I believe that even though people look and feel

4 healthy, fashion insists that they be even thinner and more

5 well-proportioned than they already are. Furthermore, if they are

6 not, then there are endless remedies such as fad diets, diet pills,

7 and health spas to help them lose the extra weight. Thus, I

8 conclude that it is not at all surprising that Americans spend

9 millions of dollars each year on these remedies to achieve their

10 goal.

REFERENTS

they — most Americans _____

_____

_____

_____

_____

_____

_____

_____

_____

Copyright © 1983 by Harcourt Brace Jovanovich, Inc. All rights reserved.

CONNECTIVES

consequently — result

_____

_____

_____

_____

Sentence Combining

Combine each group of sentences to make one sentence and write it
on the lines below. The sentences will then make a personal opinion
paragraph about city vs. country life. The vocabulary cues at the
right will help you combine the sentences.

1. **a.** I disagree with certain people.   (who)
   b. Certain people prefer country life to city life.

2. **a.** Country life is quieter and slower-paced.   (although or but or
   b. Country life is isolated and boring.   however)

3. **a.** City life is busy.   (and)
   b. City life is exciting.
   c. City life is unpredictable.

4. **a.** There is always something to do.   (because or so)
   b. You never get bored.

5. **a.** And you never know who you will meet.   (or)
   b. You never know what will happen next.

6. **a.** People from all over come to the city to shop.
   b. People from all over come to the city to visit   (and)
          family and friends.
   c. People from all over come to the city to do
          business.

7. **a.** The city provides entertainment.
   b. The city provides education.   (and or as well as)
   c. The entertainment is for people young and old.
   d. The education is for people young and old.

8. **a.** I believe something.   (that)
   b. The city is the best place to raise a family.

Copyright © 1983 by Harcourt Brace Jovanovich, Inc. All rights reserved.

_____

_____

_____

_____

_____

_____

_____

_____

_____

_____

_____

_____

Proofreading

The following version of the Reading Selection contains 10 mistakes.
The errors are faulty subject-verb agreement (2), articles (2), plural
nouns (1), pronouns (3), count/noncount nouns (1), and sentence
fragments (1). Find the mistakes and correct them.

1   In my opinion advertising is nothing. But the

2 money-making plot to control our life. Television and radio

3 commercials, as well as newspaper, magazine, and subway ads,

4 all cries out to us "BUY, BUY, BUY." I believe that there catchy

5 songs and slogans, bright attractive ads, and beautiful models

6 all conspire to sell us products they either do not want or do not

7 need. Even when we do need to buy something, we usually buy it

Copyright © 1983 by Harcourt Brace Jovanovich, Inc. All rights reserved.

8 for a wrong reason. Colorful packages and amusing ads get

9 better sale results than actual quality do. In addition, many

10 commercials are misleading or dishonest and give the public

11 false informations. It is clear to me that until we stop believing

12 everything we see and hear in advertisements, they will continue

13 to control you.

Copyright © 1983 by Harcourt Brace Jovanovich, Inc. All rights reserved.

FORMAL WRITING

Writing Topics

Choose one of the five topics below and write a personal opinion paragraph. Remember to state your topic sentence in the *introduction*, to develop your *discussion* completely, and to summarize or restate your topic sentence in the *conclusion*. Try to use personal opinion vocabulary. If you find it helpful, outline the three parts of the paragraph before writing. Write your paragraph on notebook composition paper.

1. What is your opinion of a recent movie or book?

2. What is your opinion of an important political issue in your country or in the world?

3. Can you think of a profession that should be open to only one sex? Which one? Why?

4. Do governments have the right to limit the size of families by enforcing the use of birth control? Could they enforce the law?

5. Should people be able to live and work in any country they want without the restrictions of visas and immigration papers?

Checklist

ORGANIZATION

1. Is your topic sentence in the introduction?
2. Does the discussion develop and support your topic sentence?
3. Does your conclusion summarize or restate your topic sentence?

GRAMMAR
Have you checked for errors in the following?

1. verb tense sequence
2. subject-verb agreement
3. pronoun agreement
4. articles
5. prepositions
6. sentence boundaries

VOCABULARY

1. Have you used personal opinion vocabulary to structure your paragraph?
2. Have you checked difficult words for correct spelling?

6

CLASSIFICATION

PREWRITING STRATEGIES

- Are you superstitious? Explain your answer.

- In your country how common is the belief in superstitions?

- Describe one popular superstition that gives a warning of bad luck.

- Are there any lucky or unlucky days or numbers in your country? What are they?

- Where do you think superstitions come from?

Useful vocabulary for discussion:

(to believe in) superstitions
(to be) superstitious
(to have) good or bad luck
(to be) lucky or unlucky
chance
fortune
omen
good-luck charm
witch
ghost
magic

Reading Selection

Here is a paragraph classifying superstitions about cats.

different / divisions / sign / luck / belong in or to

people who work in mines / underground places where minerals are found

evil person

divided

Superstitions about cats can be divided into two major con-trasting° categories°: cats as carriers of good luck or omens° of bad fortune°. In the theater, cats fall into° the first division because actors believe a cat brings luck to the performance. Historically, sailors at sea also considered cats as lucky, and the ship's cat was often the first to be saved in an emergency. In Great Britain black cats mean good luck, whereas people in the U.S. and some Euro-pean countries believe black cats bring bad luck. Miners° will not even say the word "cat" in the coal mines° because they think the animal is so unlucky. Some of the superstitions that portray cats as bad luck come from the days when people believed in witches°. There are many more superstitions about cats, and most of them can be classified° into these two basic categories.

Discussion Questions

1. How are cats viewed in your country?

2. Can you think of a superstition about cats? Describe it.

3. Do you think black cats are lucky or unlucky? Why?

4. Do you know any superstitions about other animals? What are they?

WRITING EXERCISES

Organization

CLASSIFICATION: The reading selection is a paragraph of *classification* that involves three basic steps: gathering information, arranging the information into categories, and omitting the information that does not fit. Here is a list of structure vocabulary that signals classification.

classification
division
category
class
section
group
kind
type
characteristic
quality
main
major
minor
basic
some of
most of
all of
to classify into
to divide into
to sort
to include
to be included in
_____ fall into _____ category
_____ can be divided into _____ classes
to be listed

Exercise 1

Here is the Reading Selection again. Study it and underline all the words and phrases that indicate classification.

Superstitions about cats can be divided into two

major contrasting categories: cats as carriers of good luck

Copyright © 1983 by Harcourt Brace Jovanovich, Inc. All rights reserved.

or omens of bad fortune. In the theater, cats fall into the first division because actors believe a cat brings luck to the performance. Historically, sailors at sea also considered cats as lucky, and the ship's cat was often the first to be saved in an emergency. In Great Britain black cats mean good luck, whereas people in the U.S. and some European countries believe black cats bring bad luck. Miners will not even say the word "cat" in the coal mines because they think the animal is so unlucky. Some of the superstitions that portray cats as bad luck come from the days when people believed in witches. There are many more superstitions about cats, and most of them can be classified into these two basic categories.

Exercise 2

Below is a list of twelve words. Arrange them into three categories and give each group a name. Be prepared to support your divisions because there are many possibilities.

friend
receipt
salesclerk
textbook
cards
examination
magazine
typewriter
teacher
cash register
notebook
radio

1. _____   _____

   _____

2. _____   _____

   _____

Copyright © 1983 by Harcourt Brace Jovanovich, Inc. All rights reserved.

3. _____   _____

_____

Exercise 3: Brainstorming

This exercise involves all three steps in the classification process.

Choose a student to act as secretary at the blackboard.

1. Write a single word on the blackboard (such as happiness or beauty). Each person in the class tells the secretary the first word he or she thinks of when hearing the word *beauty*. List all the words on the blackboard and continue adding words for about ten minutes.

2. In small groups arrange the words on the board into categories.

3. Omit all words that do not fit into any of the categories.

4. Share your categories with the rest of the class and compare. You will probably find that there are many logical ways to arrange the information you have collected on the board.

Exercise 4

MODEL PARAGRAPH: Study the following paragraph of classification. Underline the topic sentence. Circle all words and phrases that signal order by classification.

As soon as you walk into a library or bookshop, it is clear that there are many different types of books. Two major categories are fiction and nonfiction. Novels and short stories are classified as fiction while nonfiction can be divided into many more classes such as history, biography, sociology, and science. Some other kinds of books include art books, reference books, poetry, and drama. Sometimes a book may fall into more than one division. For example, a historical novel may be listed in the history section as well as the fiction section because of the histor-

Copyright © 1983 by Harcourt Brace Jovanovich, Inc. All rights reserved.

ical information it contains. Classifying books can be a difficult job, since each book has so many characteristics to consider.

Exercise 5

Choose any one of the following topic sentences and add a discussion and conclusion to make it a complete paragraph.

1.   I look for three basic qualities in a friendship.

2.   There are many different kinds of music.

3.   My classmates can be divided into three groups.

or

Write a paragraph of classification of *beauty.* Use your lists and categories to help you.

Use some vocabulary of classification to structure your paragraph. Study the list of examples and the sample paragraph above before writing. Write your paragraph on notebook paper. Fill in the outline below with your topic sentence, some details to be used in your discussion, and your concluding sentence before writing.

I.   (Topic Sentence) _____

_____

_____

II.   (Discussion)

   A. _____

_____

   B. _____

_____

   C. _____

_____

III.   (Conclusion) _____

_____

_____

Copyright © 1983 by Harcourt Brace Jovanovich, Inc. All rights reserved.

Development: Topic Sentence of the Paragraph

In a classification paragraph the topic sentence introduces the *categories or classes* discussed and developed in the rest of the paragraph. Here are some examples of possible topic sentences that introduce information about the sounds of the English language. The main idea is the same in the three sentences, but the "classification" vocabulary is different.

The sounds of the English consonants are divided into five major categories.

We can classify the sounds of the English consonants into five basic divisions.

The sounds of the English consonants fall into five major classifications.

Read each topic sentence. Write two new ones that restate the main idea but contain different "classification" vocabulary.

1. The trees of North America fall into two categories.

   a. _____

   _____

   b. _____

   _____

2. We can basically divide classical music into four periods.

   a. _____

   _____

   b. _____

   _____

3. Three main classes make up the socio-economic structure of the U.S.

   a. _____

   _____

   b. _____

   _____

Copyright © 1983 by Harcourt Brace Jovanovich, Inc. All rights reserved.

Sentence Combining

Combine each group of sentences to make one sentence, using the vocabulary cues at the right. After you combine each sentence, write it on the lines below. The sentences will make a classification paragraph.

Example: **a.** It is dangerous to put people into   (because)
                   categories.
            b. You simplify their personalities.

It is dangerous to put people into categories because you simplify their personalities.

1. **a.** It seems that way.   (that)
   b. There are two kinds of relatives.

2. **a.** The first kind is the relative you do not like.   (and)
   b. The first kind is the relative you would never choose to be part of your family.

3. **a.** My cousin William falls into that category.   (because)
   b. He has to be the most difficult person to get along with.

4. **a.** We were young.   (when)
   b. He used to tease me.   (and)
   c. He used to start fights.

5. **a.** William was usually to blame.   (even though or
   b. He would never admit it to our parents. although)

6. **a.** The second kind of relative is the one you love. (and)
   b. The second kind of relative is the one you would love even if you were not related.

7. **a.** A good example is my Uncle Julian.   (who)
   b. He was my favorite person.   (when)
   c. I was a child.

8. **a.** Uncle Julian would take me to the zoo.
   b. Uncle Julian would take me to look at the   (and)
       monkeys.   (and)
   c. Then we would imitate them.
   d. Then we would laugh at each other.

Copyright © 1983 by Harcourt Brace Jovanovich, Inc. All rights reserved.

9. **a.** I was sad or troubled.   (if or when)
   b. He would take time to talk with me.

10. **a.** Relatives like Uncle Julian help make up for
    the Williams.   (and)
    b. Relatives like Uncle Julian help make up for
    the other unlikeable relatives.

_____

_____

_____

_____

_____

_____

_____

_____

_____

_____

_____

_____

_____

_____

_____

_____

_____

Proofreading

The following version of the reading selection contains nine mistakes. The errors are faulty subject-verb agreement (1), articles (1),
plurality (1), active/passive voice (1), verb tense (1), possession (1),

Copyright © 1983 by Harcourt Brace Jovanovich, Inc. All rights reserved.

pronoun agreement (1), count/noncount nouns (1), and demonstrative adjectives (1). Find the mistakes and correct them.

1   Superstitions about cats can divide into two major

2 contrasting categories: cats as carriers of good luck or omen of

3 bad fortune. In the theater, cats fall into the first division

4 because actors believe a cat bring luck to the performance.

5 Historically, sailors at sea also consider cats as lucky, and the

6 ships cat was often the first to be saved in an emergency. In

7 Great Britain black cats mean good luck, whereas people in the

8 U.S. and some European countries believe black cats bring bad

9 luck. Miners will not even say a word "cat" in the coal mines

10 because he thinks the animal is so unlucky. Some of the

11 superstitions that portray cats as bad luck come from the days

12 when people believed in witches. There are much more

13 superstitions about cats, and most of them can be classified into

14 this two basic categories.

Copyright © 1983 by Harcourt Brace Jovanovich, Inc. All rights reserved.

FORMAL WRITING

Writing Topics

Choose one of the five topics below and write a classification paragraph. Remember to state your topic sentence in the *introduction,* to develop your *discussion* completely, and to summarize or restate your topic sentence in the *conclusion.* Try to use classification vocabulary. If you find it helpful, outline the three parts of the paragraph before writing. Write your paragraph on notebook composition paper.

1. occupations

2. sports

3. movies

4. your friends or family

5. any other topic of your choice

After you write your paragraph, use the checklist below to help you edit your paragraph. Make sure you have done everything on the list.

Checklist

ORGANIZATION
1. Is your topic sentence in the introduction?
2. Does the discussion develop and support your topic sentence?
3. Does your conclusion summarize or restate the topic sentence?

GRAMMAR
Have you checked for errors in the following?
1. verb tense sequence
2. subject-verb agreement
3. pronoun agreement
4. articles
5. prepositions
6. sentence boundaries

VOCABULARY
1. Have you used classification vocabulary to structure your paragraph?
2. Have you checked difficult words for correct spelling?

7

COMPARISON AND CONTRAST

PREWRITING STRATEGIES

- How would you express the following without the use of words?

    "I don't understand you."
    "I don't know."
    "What? I don't believe it!"
    "I'm angry."
    "I'm depressed today."

- You are at a party. Someone begins to talk with you, but you do not want to know him or her. How do you let that person know you are not interested by using body language?

- Now imagine the opposite situation. You are again at the party, and someone shyly introduces himself or herself. How do you encourage that person? How do you let him or her know that you would like to get acquainted? Describe the body language you would probably use.

Useful vocabulary for discussion:

body language
movement
motion
gesture
to (make a) gesture
eye contact
to make eye contact
to stare
facial expression
to make a face
to raise your eyebrows
to shrug your shoulders
to cross your arms/legs
to frown

Reading Selection

Here is a comparison-contrast paragraph that discusses the body language of North and South Americans.

When comparing the body language of North and South Americans, we find more differences than similarities. For example, North Americans do not prolong° eye contact during a conversation, whereas South Americans do. A person from North America usually meets the other person's eyes for a few seconds, looks away, and then back again, but a South American looks directly into the other person's eyes and considers it impolite° if he does not. Another difference is the contrast° in using hand movements while speaking. The South American uses many gestures; however, the North American uses them only occasionally°. The North and South American have more in common° when we examine the distance each maintains° from the person he is talking with. Unless there exists° a close friendship, both the North and South American stand about two to three feet from the other person. By studying the differences in body language of a group of North and South Americans, we could probably figure out where each person comes from.

make long

not polite
difference

once in a while
to be similar
keeps
is

Discussion Questions

1. Do you "talk with your hands" when you are having a conversation? In your opinion, do men or women use their hands more while talking? Explain your answer.

2. How far away do you stand while talking with a friend? With a teacher? With a stranger? With your boss?

3. What kind of eye contact do you maintain when having a conversation? Does eye contact depend on who you are talking with? Explain.

WRITING EXERCISES

Organization: Comparison and Contrast

The reading selection is organized by the relationship of *comparison-contrast*. When we *compare* and *contrast* two different things, we examine their similarities and differences. The following list gives examples of words that structure a paragraph organized by a comparison-contrast relationship.

COMPARE: to compare
comparison
similarity (between)
to be similar (to)
to be equal (to)
to be the same as
to be alike
to resemble
resemblance
just as
in the same way
to have *something* in common

CONTRAST: to contrast
contrast
difference (between)
to be different (from)
to differ (from)
less than, more than, *bigger* than, etc.
unlike
on the other hand
however
although
nevertheless
while
whereas
but

Exercise 1

Here is the Reading Selection again. Study it and underline all words and phrases that indicate comparison-contrast.

When comparing the body language of North and

South Americans, we find more differences than

similarities. For example, North Americans do not prolong

eye contact during a conversation, whereas South Amer-

Copyright © 1983 by Harcourt Brace Jovanovich, Inc. All rights reserved.

icans do. A person from North America usually meets the other person's eyes for a few seconds, looks away, and then back again; but a South American looks directly into the other person's eyes and considers it impolite if he does not. Another difference is the contrast in using hand movements while speaking. The South American uses many gestures; however, the North American uses them only occasionally. The North and South American have more in common when we examine the distance each maintains from the person he is talking with. Unless there exists a close friendship, both the North and South American stand about two to three feet from the other person. By studying the differences in body language of a group of North and South Americans, we could probably figure out where each person comes from.

Exercise 2

Using the information from the chart below, write *three statements of comparison* and *three statements of contrast*. Try to use the structure vocabulary from the above lists. For example:

The population of Great Britain is almost the same as that of Italy.

While Italy has only one major language spoken, Switzerland has three.

Country	Location	Population	Major Language(s) Spoken
China	Asia	900,000,000	Mandarin and Cantonese
France	Europe	53,000,000	French
Haiti	Caribbean	5,000,000	French and Creole
Soviet Union	Eurasia	255,000,000	Russian
United States	North America	212,000,000	English
Italy	Europe	57,000,000	Italian
Costa Rica	Central America	2,000,000	Spanish
Great Britain	Europe	56,000,000	English
Morocco	Africa	18,000,000	Arabic
Switzerland	Europe	7,000,000	French, German, and Italian

Copyright © 1983 by Harcourt Brace Jovanovich, Inc. All rights reserved.

COMPARISON:

1. _____

_____

_____

2. _____

_____

_____

3. _____

_____

_____

CONTRAST:

1. _____

_____

_____

2. _____

_____

_____

3. _____

_____

_____

Exercise 3

MODEL PARAGRAPH: Study the following comparison-contrast paragraph. Underline the topic sentence. Circle all words and phrases that signal a comparison-contrast relationship.

Researchers have found that parents view boy babies and girl babies differently as early as the first week of life. Little girls are said to be unlike boys in both facial characteristics and personality. Boy babies are usually bigger than girl babies and are actually described as stronger and

Copyright © 1983 by Harcourt Brace Jovanovich. Inc. All rights reserved.

more alert than little girls. On the other hand, little girls are seen as sweeter, gentler, and more passive than boys. Although two infants may look alike or be equally fragile, parents handle boy babies with less care than girls. Even though little boys and girls seem different to their parents as early as one day old, these differences do not necessarily exist in reality.

Exercise 4

Write a paragraph comparing and contrasting one of the following pairs:

1. your mother and father
2. yourself and a friend
3. a brother and a sister
4. the educational systems of two countries

Fill in the outline below with your topic sentence, some details to be used in your discussion, and your concluding sentence. Remember to use some comparison-contrast vocabulary to structure your paragraph. Study the list of examples and the model paragraph above before writing. Write your paragraph on notebook paper.

1. (Topic Sentence) _____

_____

_____

II. (Discussion)

  A. _____

_____

  B. _____

_____

  C. _____

_____

Copyright © 1983 by Harcourt Brace Jovanovich, Inc. All rights reserved.

III. (Conclusion) ———————————————————————

———————————————————————————————

———————————————————————————————

Development: Coherence of the Paragraph

Study the *referents* and *connectives* in Chapter Five in the Development section. *Referents* are words that substitute for other words: like "he" for John. *Connectives* are words that link ideas by defining their relationship to one another: connectives of addition, contrast, time and result.

Read the paragraph below and locate all the referents and connectives. Write them in the lines provided. For the referents, write down what the referent refers to. For the connectives, write down what type it is.

> Both film and theater are effective means of dramatic expression, but each has different qualities that make it a popular art form. In a film, the audience can experience close-up photography and actual changes in time and location. People can see small changes in facial expression, new and different geography, and real events in nature. Although plays do not offer the same, they do encourage a close involvement between the audience and actors. Actors sense the audience's reaction and then alter their voices and actions accordingly. This quality of intimacy makes seeing a play an exciting experience and as a result causes many people to prefer the theater to the cinema.

Referents   *Connectives*

——————————————   ——————————————

——————————————   ——————————————

——————————————   ——————————————

——————————————   ——————————————

——————————————

Copyright © 1983 by Harcourt Brace Jovanovich, Inc. All rights reserved.

Sentence Combining

Combine each group of sentences to make one sentence and write the sentence on the lines below. The sentences will make a comparison-contrast paragraph. The vocabulary cues at the right will help you.

1. **a.** I like Italian cooking.   (and)
   b. I like Chinese cooking.   (even though or but)
   c. They are very different.

2. **a.** They are both spicy.   (although)
   b. Italian cooks use garlic and oregano.   (while)
   c. Chinese cooks often use ginger and hot pepper.

3. **a.** The Italians use a lot of tomato sauce.   (unlike . . . who)
   b. The Chinese use bean sauce.
   c. The Chinese use soy sauce.   (and)
   d. The Chinese use duck sauce.

4. **a.** An Italian meal is usually served with wine.   (however or while)
   b. A Chinese meal is usually served with tea.

5. **a.** No Italian meal is complete without something.   (whereas or but)
   b. The something is a loaf of delicious Italian bread.
   c. The Chinese never serve bread of any kind.

6. **a.** Another difference between Italian and Chinese cooking is this.   (that)
   b. Most Italian dishes are baked.   (while)
   c. Most Chinese dishes are cooked in hot oil.

7. **a.** Also, Italians eat a lot of pasta.   (and or while)
   b. Chinese people eat a lot of vegetables.

8. **a.** They are not alike.   (although)
   b. I enjoy Italian food.   (and)
   c. I enjoy Chinese food.

_____

_____

_____

Copyright © 1983 by Harcourt Brace Jovanovich, Inc. All rights reserved.

_____

_____

_____

_____

_____

_____

_____

_____

_____

_____

_____

_____

Proofreading

The following version of the Reading Selection contains ten mistakes: articles (1), subject-verb agreement (2), verb forms (1), plurality (1), adverb (1), pronoun agreement (1), preposition (1), possession (1), and sentence fragments (1). Find the mistakes and correct them.

1   When comparing the body language of North and South

2 Americans, we find more differences than similarity. For

3 example, North Americans do not prolong eye contact during the

4 conversation, whereas South Americans do. A person from

5 North America usually meets the other persons eyes for a few

6 seconds, look away, and then back again: but a South American

Copyright © 1983 by Harcourt Brace Jovanovich, Inc. All rights reserved.

7 looks direct into the other person's eyes and consider it impolite

8 if he does not. Another difference is the contrast in using hand

9 movements while speak. The South American uses many

10 gestures; however, the North American uses it only occasionally.

11 The North and South American have more in common. When we

12 examine the distance each maintains from the person he is

13 talking with. Unless there exists a close friendship, both the

14 North and South American stand about two to three feet of the

15 other person. By studying the differences in body language of a

16 group of North and South Americans, we could probably figure

17 out where each person came from.

Copyright © 1983 by Harcourt Brace Jovanovich, Inc. All rights reserved.

FORMAL WRITING

Writing Topics

Choose one of the three topics below or one of your own and write a comparison-contrast paragraph about the topic. Remember to state your topic sentence in the *introduction,* to develop your *discussion* completely, and to summarize or restate your main idea in the *conclusion.* Try to use the comparison-contrast vocabulary you have been practicing in this chapter. If you want, outline the three parts of the paragraph before writing. Write your paragraph on notebook composition paper.

1. yourself now and five years ago

2. two different places you have lived

3. two different forms of government

After you write your paragraph, use the checklist below to help you edit your paragraph. Make sure you have done everything on the list.

Checklist

ORGANIZATION

1. Is your topic sentence in the introduction?
2. Does the discussion develop and support your topic sentence?
3. Does your conclusion summarize or restate the topic sentence?

GRAMMAR
Have you checked for errors in the following?

1. verb tense sequence
2. subject-verb agreement
3. pronoun agreement
4. articles
5. prepositions
6. sentence boundaries

VOCABULARY

1. Have you used comparison-contrast vocabulary to structure your paragraph?
2. Have you checked difficult words for correct spelling?

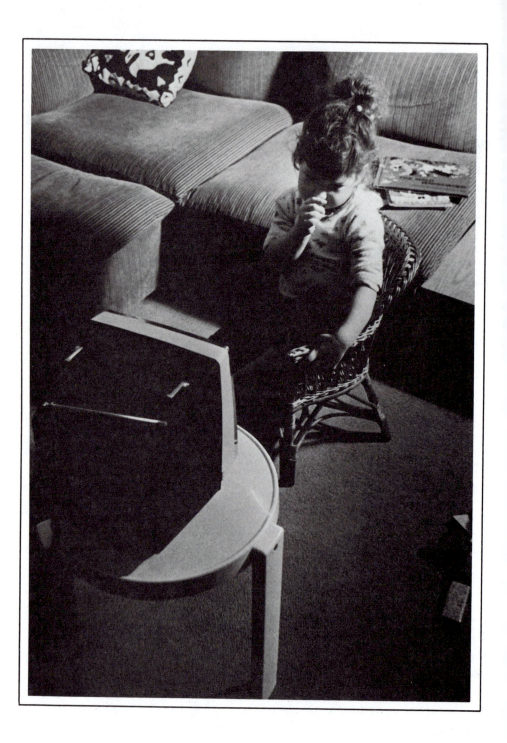

8

CAUSE AND EFFECT

PREWRITING STRATEGIES

- How much time do you spend watching television each day?

- If given the choice between reading a good book, seeing friends, or watching television, which would you choose?

- Why do you think television has been named the "boob tube" in recent years? What do you think this means?

- Describe the television networks in your country. How many channels are there? What types of shows do they broadcast? How many hours per day are programs on the air?

Useful vocabulary for discussion:

TV, television
channel
station
to broadcast
broadcast
commercials
to brainwash
to influence
to be violent
program
  comedies
  documentaries
  dramas (crime, adventure)
  game shows
  talk shows
soap operas
viewer
audience

Reading Selection

The following is a cause-and-effect paragraph that discusses the harmful effects television has on children.

famous
very big
quiet, inactive
people who study behavior

originality

too much
angry, violent
copy
as a result

TV heroes
grown

When the television was invented in 1923, parents had no idea of the harmful effects this celebrated° invention would one day have on children. Because of the tremendous° amount of time children spend watching TV, they become passive° observers. Child psychologists° say that children learn best by doing, not by watching. As a result, television has a negative effect on children's learning abilities and their creativity.° Since children spend more time in front of the TV and less time behind a good book, their reading abilities have also suffered. Another harmful effect of television is caused by the excessive° violence in many popular programs. Studies show that aggressive° behavior in children is a direct result of this violence. Young people imitate° the behavior they see on TV. Consequently°, youngsters have been known to "fly" out of windows like Superman and kill their enemies like Kojak.° For all these reasons, television has evolved° from the miracle it once was into the monster it is today.

Discussion Questions

1. In the Reading Selection the writer stated that children imitate the violence they see on television. What other kinds of behavior on TV do viewers imitate? Is imitation always harmful? Why or why not?

2. Can you think of any TV stars who are imitated by the audience? Who are they? What do you think makes them attractive?

3. Compare the real world with how TV portrays it. How do the differences affect the viewer? What problems does the viewer who lives in the make-believe world of TV face in actual everyday life?

WRITING EXERCISES

Organization: Cause and Effect

The Reading Selection is organized by a cause-and-effect relationship. The *cause* is something that happens. When something happens, it affects someone, something, or a situation. The results of the cause are called the *effects*. The following list of words structure a cause-and-effect paragraph.

If . . ., then . . .
because (of)
since
due to
so, thus
therefore
consequently
as a consequence
for this reason
the reason for
to cause
to be the cause of
to have an effect on
to be the effect of
as a result
to result in
to be the result of

Exercise 1

Here is the Reading Selection again. Study it and underline all words and phrases that indicate cause and effect.

When the television was invented in 1923, parents had no idea of the harmful effects this celebrated invention would one day have on children. Because of the tremendous amount of time children spend watching TV, they become passive observers. Child psychologists say that children learn best by doing, not by watching. As a result, television has a negative effect on children's learn-

Copyright © 1983 by Harcourt Brace Jovanovich, Inc. All rights reserved.

ing abilities and their creativity. Since children spend more time in front of the TV and less time behind a good book, their reading abilities have also suffered. Another harmful effect of television is caused by the excessive violence in many popular programs. Studies show that aggressive behavior in children is a direct result of this violence. Young people imitate the behavior they see on TV. Consequently youngsters have been known to "fly" out of windows like Superman and kill their enemies like Kojak. For all these reasons, television has evolved from the miracle it once was into the monster it is today.

Exercise 2

Below is a topic sentence stating a cause-and-effect relationship and a list of data to support it. Write four statements of cause and effect using the data below.

TOPIC SENTENCE

Because of their life style and diet, a group of people in the southern part of the Soviet Union have discovered the secret to longevity.*

DATA

1. expectation of a long life
2. respect for the elderly
3. simple life with no stress
4. bathing in cold mountain streams
5. a regular and active sex life
6. no overeating
7. red wine with every meal
8. no smoking

1. _____

    _____

    _____

*a long life

Copyright © 1983 by Harcourt Brace Jovanovich, Inc. All rights reserved.

2. _____

_____

_____

3. _____

_____

_____

4. _____

_____

_____

Exercise 3

MODEL PARAGRAPH: Study the following cause-and-effect paragraph. Underline the topic sentence. Circle all words and phrases that signal a cause-and-effect relationship.

At the beginning of the century Wareham was a sleepy, coastal village, but a sudden growth in tourism resulted in the changes that have made Wareham a busy, commercial town. Today as you drive down the main street, you see an endless row of hamburger places souvenir shops, and motels. Due to the amount of people who vacation on the coast, prices at restaurants and motels are very high. In addition, the rise in tourism has consequently caused heavy summer traffic and increased the amount of car accidents. Even though some of the changes are depressing, a positive effect of tourism is the number of jobs that has been created. Because of the vacationers, the people of Wareham enjoy a more stable economy. For this reason the town is growing each year and no longer resembles the Wareham of many years ago.

Copyright © 1983 by Harcourt Brace Jovanovich, Inc. All rights reserved.

Exercise 4

Write a cause-and-effect paragraph on one of the following topics:

1. how an important event changed your life
2. how smoking affects one's health
3. how television affects children's performance in school

Fill in the outline below with your topic sentence, some details to be used in your discussion, and your conclusion. Study the list of cause-and-effect structure vocabulary before writing, and try to use some in your paragraph.

I.   (Topic Sentence) _____

_____

_____

II. (Discussion)

    A. _____

_____

    B. _____

_____

    C. _____

_____

III. (Conclusion) _____

_____

_____

Development: Unity of the Paragraph

Below are topic sentences followed by four discussion sentences that should support them. Find the statement that does not support the topic sentence and circle it.

1. Environmentalists fear that nuclear energy will one day destroy us.

   a. Scientists have not discovered a safe way to dispose of radioactive waste.

Copyright © 1983 by Harcourt Brace Jovanovich, Inc. All rights reserved.

    b. A nuclear bomb could kill millions of people and cause disease and deformity in later generations.

    c. Because of limited energy resources, scientists are studying the possibilities of nuclear power.

    d. A nuclear plant melt down would threaten the lives of people, plants, animals, and their offspring in the affected area.

2. As a result of the invention of the telephone the world has enjoyed many benefits.

    a. Contact with family and friends who live far away has been made possible.

    b. Because of the many services the telephone offers, people have to pay very high phone bills each month.

    c. The telephone has contributed greatly to efficient communication in the business world.

    d. Another result of telephone communication is the contact now possible across oceans and between continents.

Sentence Combining

Combine each group of sentences to make one sentence. After you combine each group, write the sentence on the lines below. The sentences will make a cause-and-effect paragraph. The vocabulary cues at the right will help you.

1. **a.** I never had a realistic fear for dangerous   (since)
        situations.
   b. I nearly experienced a horrible death.

2. **a.** I was always ready for an adventure.   (even though)
   b. Many people would warn me of potential
        danger.

3. **a.** But one confrontation with a shark was   (and)
      enough to cure me of being foolish.
   b. But one confrontation with a shark was
      enough to cure me of taking risks.

4. **a.** My friends and I were vacationing in the   (because)
      Caribbean.
   b. We were all interested in deep-sea diving.

5. **a.** We were warned to avoid diving on the south   (although)
      side of the island.
   b. I wanted to explore that area.   (because)
   c. A treasure ship had once disappeared there.

Copyright © 1983 by Harcourt Brace Jovanovich, Inc. All rights reserved.

6. **a.** I suggested a diving expedition.   (when)
    b. I could not interest any of my friends.

7. **a.** So one morning very early I gathered all my   (and)
        diving gear.
    b. So one morning very early I drove to the
        southern coast of the island.

8. **a.** I had been in the water only five minutes.   (after)
    b. I saw a shark about fifty feet away from me.

9. **a.** Fear ran through my whole body.   (and)
    b. I could not move at first.

10. **a.** I regained some sense.   (when)
    b. I quickly swam to the surface of the water.

11. **a.** Luckily there were some fisherman in a small   (who)
        boat nearby.
    b. They came to my rescue.

12. **a.** For one terrible moment I watched the boat   (and)
        approach me.
    b. For one terrible moment I watched the shark
        approach me.

13. **a.** I am here to tell the story.   (and consequently)
    b. I have stopped taking crazy risks.

_____

_____

_____

_____

_____

_____

_____

_____

_____

_____

Copyright © 1983 by Harcourt Brace Jovanovich, Inc. All rights reserved.

_____

_____

_____

_____

_____

_____

_____

_____

_____

_____

_____

Proofreading

The following version of the Reading Selection contains twelve mistakes: verb tense (2), plurality (2), fragments (1), run-on sentences (1), articles (2), possession (1), word forms (1), homonyms (example: no/know) (1), and possessive adjectives (1). Find the mistakes and correct them.

1 When the television was invented in 1923, parents have no

2 idea of the harmful effects this celebrated invention would one

3 day have on children. Because of the tremendous amount of

4 times children spend watching TV. They become passive

5 observers. Child psychologists say that children learn best by

6 doing, not by watching, as a result, television has negative effect

7 on childrens learning abilities and their creativity. Since

8 children spend more time in front of the TV and less time behind

Copyright © 1983 by Harcourt Brace Jovanovich, Inc. All rights reserved.

9 the good book, his reading abilities have also suffered. Another

10 harmful effect of television is caused by the excessive violence in

11 many popular programs. Studies show that aggression behavior

12 in children is a direct result of this violence. Young children

13 imitate the behavior they see on TV. Consequently, youngsters

14 have been known to "fly" out of windows like Superman and kill

15 there enemies like Kojak. For all these reason, television has

16 evolve from the miracle it once was into the monster it is today.

Copyright © 1983 by Harcourt Brace Jovanovich, Inc. All rights reserved.

FORMAL WRITING

Writing Topics

Choose one of the three topics below or one of your own and write a cause-and-effect paragraph about the topic. Remember to state your topic sentence in the *introduction*, to develop your *discussion* completely, and to summarize or restate your main idea in the *conclusion*. Try to use the cause and effect vocabulary you have been practicing. If you want, outline the three parts of the paragraph before writing. Write your paragraph on notebook composition paper.

1. how a person changed your life

2. the effect of fads on the clothing industry

3. the effect of technology on the environment
    (example: the effect of factory and automobile exhaust on the
    air quality)

After you write your paragraph, use the checklist below to help you edit your paragraph. Make sure you have done everything on the list.

Checklist

ORGANIZATION

1. Is your topic sentence in the introduction?
2. Does the discussion develop and support your topic sentence?
3. Does your conclusion summarize or restate the topic sentence?

GRAMMAR
Have you checked for errors in the following?

1. verb tense sequence
2. subject-verb agreement
3. pronoun agreement
4. articles
5. prepositions
6. sentence boundaries

VOCABULARY

1. Have you used cause-and-effect vocabulary to structure your paragraph?
2. Have you checked difficult words for correct spelling?

9

PROBLEM-SOLUTION

PREWRITING STRATEGIES

- Do you think a utopia could ever exist on earth? If so, under what conditions? What would it be like?

- Do you know of any utopias planned or attempted in the past? Describe them.

- Why do you think people throughout history have tried to create utopias? What has motivated them?

Useful vocabulary for discussion:

utopia
utopian
society
commune, community
social structure
political structure
economic structure
freedom
to rule
ruler
to serve
servant
ideal
idealist
perfect
perfection

Reading Selection

Here is a problem-solution paragraph about a utopia.

perfect society   In 1516 Sir Thomas More wrote *Utopia*°, his plan for the perfect world. More thought the political and social structure of each
circle   city should revolve° around the family. Every year thirty families
officer or leader   would elect an official° to govern them. Every person would learn a
occupation   trade° that would be passed down in the family. Sir Thomas felt that women should serve their husbands and be ruled by them.
capitalism   Economically, he feared that private ownership° would be dangerous, and so he planned a society with no private property or money. All goods would be exchanged freely, and all citizens would
selfishness   live as one big family. In order to discourage greediness°, he
valuable jewels   suggested that pearls and diamonds° be given to children as toys. More, a true idealist, thought this would be the best of all possible worlds.

Discussion Questions

1. Do you think Thomas More's utopia would be successful today? Why or why not?

2. What do you like best about his plan for a perfect world?

3. Which of the suggestions do you disagree with? Why?

WRITING EXERCISES

Organization: Problem-Solution

The reading selection offers one *solution* to the *problems* of society. It is structured with words and phrases that signal problem solving. Below is a list of vocabulary to structure a problem-solving paragraph.

to think
to suggest (I would suggest . . .)
to plan (I would plan . . .)
to prevent (I would prevent . . .)
to demand (I would demand . . .)
you should
it would be better, dangerous, beneficial, helpful, etc.
it would be a good idea if (to) . . .
one solution would be . . .
another solution would be . . .
proposal
plan
strategy

Exercise 1

Here is the Reading Selection again. Study it and underline all words and phrases that indicate problem-solution.

In 1516 Sir Thomas More wrote *Utopia*, his plan for the perfect world. More thought the political and social structure of each city should revolve around the family. Every year thirty families would elect an official to govern them. Every person would learn a trade that would be passed down in the family. Sir Thomas felt that women should serve their husbands and be ruled by them. Economically, he feared that private ownership would be dangerous, and so he planned a society with no private property or money. All goods would be exchanged freely,

Copyright © 1983 by Harcourt Brace Jovanovich, Inc. All rights reserved.

and all citizens would live as one big family. In order to discourage greediness, he suggested that pearls and diamonds be given to children as toys. More, a true idealist, thought this would be the best of all possible worlds.

Exercise 2

In small groups:
a. decide on the three major problems in the world today.
b. plan a utopia that would solve or eliminate these problems.
c. outline your utopian solutions below.

First problem: _____

_____

Utopian solution: _____

_____

_____

Second problem: _____

_____

Utopian solution: _____

_____

_____

Third problem: _____

_____

Utopian solution: _____

_____

_____

Exercise 3

MODEL PARAGRAPH: Study the following problem-solving paragraph. Underline the topic sentence. Circle all words and phrases that signal problem-solution.

Copyright © 1983 by Harcourt Brace Jovanovich, Inc. All rights reserved.

The recent strike by bus drivers and workers has put one city in a state of chaos. People are having trouble getting to work, and stores are suffering from the lack of shoppers. To help the situation I suggest that we use other forms of transportation in a systematic and logical way. If we drive to work, we should find others who need a ride and use one car for four people. This strategy of car sharing would also be effective in regard to travel by taxi. In addition, it would be helpful if people who live close to work could create two work shifts: one from 5 A.M. to 1 P.M. and the other from 1 P.M. to 8 P.M. This would lessen traffic during the usual rush hours. All of the above proposals could help us during this difficult transportation crisis.

Exercise 4

Write a problem-solution paragraph on one of the following topics:

1. Discuss one of the problems your group chose in Exercise 2 and how you would solve it.

2. Disposal of nuclear waste

3. A problem in your life

Fill in the outline below with your topic sentence, some details to be used in your discussion, and your conclusion. Study the list of problem-solution vocabulary before writing, and try to use some in your paragraph.

I.   (Topic Sentence) _____

_____

_____

II. (Discussion)

A. _____

_____

Copyright © 1983 by Harcourt Brace Jovanovich, Inc. All rights reserved.

    B. _____

_____

    C. _____

_____

III. (Conclusion) _____

_____

_____

Development: Completeness of the Paragraph

The following paragraph is incomplete. State the problem and solution below and answer the questions.

> Joan Anderson was a working mother with a problem that her mother-in-law helped to solve. When her baby girl was a year old, Joan decided to return to work three days a week. The problem was that Joan could not find a babysitter. One solution was to hire a retired homemaker, but Joan's husband was against this plan. He felt it would be better and cheaper to have his mother watch the baby. Joan thought this was a good idea, but her mother-in-law was only available two days a week. The baby loves her grandmother, so everyone was happy with the solution.

1. Problem: _____

_____

_____

2. Solution: _____

_____

_____

3. Why is this solution incomplete? Write a sentence completing the solution.

_____

_____

_____

Copyright © 1983 by Harcourt Brace Jovanovich, Inc. All rights reserved.

Sentence Combining

Combine each group of sentences to make one sentence and write it on the lines below. The sentences will make a problem-solution paragraph. The vocabulary cues at the right will help you.

1. **a.** Four friends were trying to decide on a vacation.
   b. The vacation would satisfy everyone.
   (that)

2. **a.** Mike loved to swim, surf, and sail.
   b. He wanted to go to the seashore.
   c. He could enjoy his favorite sports.
   (so or and)
   (where)

3. **a.** Robert did not agree with his idea.
   b. He was an art student.
   c. He wanted to go to Washington, D.C.
   d. He wanted to visit the museums.
   (because)
   (and)

4. **a.** Eric thought so.
   b. It would be better to leave the cities behind.
   c. It would be better to go to the mountains.
   d. It was quiet and peaceful.
   (that)
   (and)
   (where)

5. **a.** Sam wanted to travel cross-country.
   b. He wanted to see as much as possible.
   c. He disagreed with everyone.
   (because)
   (and)

6. **a.** The four discussed their problem endlessly.
   b. The four could not come to a conclusion.
   (but or yet)

7. **a.** It seemed so.
   b. There was no happy compromise.
   (that)

8. **a.** One person made a suggestion.
   b. Another person would be dissatisfied.
   (if . . . then)

9. **a.** Finally, they came to the conclusion.
   b. They would have to take their vacations separately.
   (that)

_____

_____

_____

_____

Copyright © 1983 by Harcourt Brace Jovanovich, Inc. All rights reserved.

_____

_____

_____

_____

_____

_____

_____

_____

_____

_____

_____

Proofreading

The following version of the Reading Selection contains ten mistakes: verb tense (1), plurality (2), articles (1), word forms (1), homonyms (1), and pronoun referents (4). Find the mistakes and correct them.

1   In 1516 Sir Thomas More wrote *Utopia*, his plan for the

2 perfect world. More thought the political and social structure of

3 each cities should revolve around a family. Every year thirty

4 families would elect an official to govern it. Every person would

5 learn a trade who would be passed down in the family. Sir

6 Thomas feels that women should serve there husbands and be

7 ruled by them. Economically, he feared that private ownership

Copyright © 1983 by Harcourt Brace Jovanovich, Inc. All rights reserved.

8 would be danger, and so he planned a society with no private

9 property or money. All goods would be exchanged freely, and all

10 citizens would live as one big family. In order to discourage

11 greediness, they suggested that pearls and diamonds be given to

12 childrens as toys. More, a true idealist, thought these would be

13 the best of all possible worlds.

Copyright © 1983 by Harcourt Brace Jovanovich, Inc. All rights reserved.

FORMAL WRITING

Writing Topics

Choose one of the four topics below or one of your own and write a problem-solution paragraph about the topic. Remember to state your topic sentence in the *introduction,* to develop your *discussion* completely, and to summarize your main idea in the *conclusion.* Try to use the problem-solution vocabulary you have been practicing. If you want, outline the three parts of the paragraph before writing. Write your paragraph on notebook paper.

1. overpopulation

2. a problem at your school or job

3. unemployment

4. the role of elderly people in society

After you write your paragraph, use the checklist below to help you edit your paragraph. Make sure you have done everything on the list.

Checklist

ORGANIZATION

1. Is your topic sentence in your introduction?
2. Does the discussion develop and support your topic sentence?
3. Does your conclusion summarize or restate your topic sentence?

GRAMMAR
Have you checked for errors in the following?

1. verb tense sequence
2. subject-verb agreement
3. pronoun agreement
4. articles
5. prepositions
6. sentence boundaries

VOCABULARY

1. Have you used problem-solution vocabulary to structure your paragraph?
2. Have you checked difficult words for spelling mistakes?

10

COMPARISON AND CONTRAST

PREWRITING STRATEGIES

- What determines the differences in people's accents? Why do people pronounce certain sounds and words differently?

- How does your speech differ from someone of your grandparents' generation? Give some examples.

- What age group uses more slang than the others? Why do slang expressions change through the years?

- Who uses more polite language? Men? Women? Old people? Young people?

Useful vocabulary for discussion:

speech
accent
pronunciation
to pronounce
grammar
vocabulary
slang
swear words
euphemisms
polite
impolite, rude
formal
informal
idiomatic

Reading Selection

The following is a comparison-contrast paragraph that discusses the differences in how men and women speak.

Although English is spoken by both men and women, the two sexes do not actually use the language similarly. Recorded utterances° reveal certain differences between male and female speech that suggest fundamental° psychological differences. For example, men tend° to use the imperative when asking someone to do something. (Example: Close the door). In contrast, women usually use polite forms instead. (Example: Would you close the door?) Another dissimilarity is the use of tag questions. (Example: It's a beautiful day, isn't it?) A woman adds tag questions more often to the end of statements than a man does, as if she needs verbal° affirmation° from the person she is talking with. Vocabulary usage also distinguishes° the language of men and women. A man might be considered unmanly if he uses adjectives like "lovely" and "divine" whereas they are perfectly acceptable for women. These examples of dissimilarities only hint at° the far-reaching differences in the way men and women speak.

(margin notes:)
speech
basic
are likely

spoken / agreement
shows the difference between

suggest

Discussion Questions

1. If you read a transcription of a conversation between a man and a woman, could you tell who was speaking? What clues might help you?

2. In your native language is there a difference in the way men and women speak? Explain by giving examples.

3. Why do you think differences exist between the way men and women speak?

WRITING EXERCISES

Organization: Comparison and Contrast

The Reading Selection is organized by a comparison-contrast relationship. In Chapter 7 you studied comparison-contrast, and you can review the structure vocabulary in that chapter. Here are some additional vocabulary words that you can use when writing comparisons and contrasts.

similarly
likewise
still
otherwise
dissimilarly
on the contrary

Exercise 1

Here is the Reading Selection again. Study it and underline all words and phrases that indicate comparison-contrast.

Although English is spoken by both men and women, the two sexes do not actually use the language similarly. Recorded utterances reveal certain differences between male and female speech that suggest fundamental psychological differences. For example, men tend to use the imperative when asking someone to do something. (Example: Close the door). In contrast, women usually use polite forms instead. (Example: Would you close the door?) Another dissimilarity is the use of tag questions. (Example: It's a beautiful day, isn't it?) A woman adds tag questions more often to the end of statements than a man does, as if she needs verbal affirmation from the person she is talking with. Vocabulary usage also distinguishes the language of men and women. A man might be consid-

Copyright © 1983 by Harcourt Brace Jovanovich, Inc. All rights reserved.

ered unmanly if he uses adjectives like "lovely" and "divine" whereas they are perfectly acceptable for women. These examples of dissimilarities only hint at the far-reaching differences in the way men and women speak.

Exercise 2

Study the following information about the three leisure time activities below. Each list describes the characteristics of each activity. Then write three statements of comparison and three statements of contrast about the activities.

Playing the Piano	Playing Tennis	Making Pottery
mental exercise	physical exercise	creative
solitary/social activity	social activity	solitary activity
noncompetitive	competitive	noncompetitive
expense: instrument and lessons	expense: equipment and courts	expense: materials, but pots can be sold

1. _____

_____

_____

2. _____

_____

_____

3. _____

_____

_____

Exercise 3

MODEL PARAGRAPH: Study the following comparison-contrast paragraph. Underline the topic sentence. Circle all words and phrases that signal a comparison-contrast relationship.

    The American car of the 1980s is quite different from its predecessors. The most striking difference is the size. While the old models were large and spacious, the newer

Copyright © 1983 by Harcourt Brace Jovanovich, Inc. All rights reserved.

ones are smaller and more compact. In the past, cars were also constructed of heavier materials. Nowadays lightweight aluminum and plastic have replaced the heavyweight metals of yesterday. Engines are now more fuel efficient. Ten years ago the average American car got ten miles per gallon to compete in the market. Many of these differences are advantageous to today's driver, but unfortunately these smaller, lighter cars are not as safe if an accident occurs.

Exercise 4

Write a comparison-contrast paragraph on one of the following topics:

1. two teachers you have had
2. the newspaper versus the television news
3. English and your native language

Fill in the outline below with your topic sentence, some details in your discussion, and your conclusion. Study the list of comparison-contrast vocabulary before writing, and try to use some in your paragraph.

I. (Topic Sentence) _____

_____

_____

II. (Discussion)

   A. _____

_____

   B. _____

_____

   C. _____

_____

III. (Conclusion) _____

_____

_____

Copyright © 1983 by Harcourt Brace Jovanovich, Inc. All rights reserved.

Development: Topic Sentence of the Paragraph

The following two paragraphs are complete except for the topic sentence. Study each and write an appropriate topic sentence.

1. _____

_____

_____

Although the subway is faster, and the fare is the same, I prefer the bus for a few reasons. Buses are usually cleaner and less noisy than trains. And while both are popular in the city, the bus is often less crowded. Unlike a trip on the subway, a bus ride can be lively and interesting since you can look out the window. In general, if you are not in a hurry, a bus ride is more enjoyable than a subway.

2. _____

_____

_____

For one thing after I transferred, I realized that my new school would be more difficult. While I had always been an A student before, I now receive Bs and B minuses on my papers and exams. Another difference is that the students seem older and less friendly. In my old school there were many social clubs and dances, whereas here there are none at all. Even the campus looks different with its modern buildings and spotless lawns. It is clear that my new school is very different from the old one.

Sentence Combining

Combine each group of sentences to make one sentence and write the sentence on the lines below. The sentences will make a cause-and-effect paragraph. The vocabulary cues at the right will help you.

1.   **a.** I love both my parents equally.   (although)
      b. They are very different.

Copyright © 1983 by Harcourt Brace Jovanovich, Inc. All rights reserved.

2. a. My mother is a relaxed person.   (and)
    b. My mother is a reassuring person.   (while)
    c. My father is a nervous person.   (and)
    d. My father is a worrisome person.

3. a. My mother graduated from college.   (but)
    b. My father never even finished high school.   (because)
    c. He had to work to support his family.

4. a. He has been working hard ever since.   (whereas)
    b. My mother stopped working.   (after)
    c. They were married.

5. a. My mother loves to read and entertain.   (but)
    b. My father prefers crossword puzzles.   (and)
    c. My father prefers solitude.

6. My parents also look very different.

7. a. My mother is tall.
    b. My mother is slender.
    c. My mother is a brunette.   (; however)
    d. My father is short.
    e. My father is stocky.
    f. My father is a redhead.

8. a. They seem so different.   (because)
    b. They surprise a lot of people.   (but)
    c. My brother and I think something.   (that)
    d. They are a perfect match.

_____

_____

_____

_____

_____

_____

_____

_____

_____

_____

Copyright © 1983 by Harcourt Brace Jovanovich, Inc. All rights reserved.

_____

_____

_____

_____

_____

Proofreading

The following version of the Reading Selection contains ten mistakes: subject-verb agreement (1), verb forms (2), pronoun agreement (1), adverbs (1), plurality (2), comparatives (1), prepositions (1), and sentence fragments (1).

1   Although English is spoken by both man and women, the

2 two sexes do not actually use the language similar. Recorded

3 utterances reveal certain differences between male and female

4 speech that suggests fundamental psychological differences. For

5 example, men tend to use the imperative when asking someone

6 do something. (Example: Close the door.) In contrast, woman

7 usually use polite forms instead. (Example: Would you close the

8 door?) Another dissimilarity is the use of tag questions.

9 (Example: Is a beautiful day, isn't it?) A woman adds tag

10 questions oftener to the end of statements than a man does. As if

11 she needs verbal affirmation from the person she is talking with.

12 Vocabulary usage also distinguishes the language of men and

13 women. A man might considered unmanly if they use adjectives

Copyright © 1983 by Harcourt Brace Jovanovich, Inc. All rights reserved.

14 like "lovely" and "divine" whereas they are perfectly acceptable

15 with women. These examples of dissimilarities only hint at the

16 far-reaching differences in the way men and women speak.

Copyright © 1983 by Harcourt Brace Jovanovich, Inc. All rights reserved.

FORMAL WRITING

Writing Topics

Choose one of the three topics below or one of your own and write a comparison-contrast paragraph. Remember to state your topic sentence in the *introduction*, to develop your *discussion* completely, and to summarize or restate your main idea in the *conclusion*. Try to use the comparison-contrast vocabulary you have been practicing. If you want, outline the three parts of the paragraph before writing. Write your paragraph on notebook composition paper.

1.   the professional life of an artist and a businessman

2.   two political leaders in the world

3.   two restaurants you go to

After you write your paragraph, use the checklist below to help you edit your paragraph. Make sure you have done everything on the list.

Checklist

ORGANIZATION

1.   Is your topic sentence in the introduction?
2.   Does the discussion develop and support your topic sentence?
3.   Does your conclusion summarize or restate the topic sentence?

GRAMMAR
Have you checked for errors in the following?

1.   verb tense sequence
2.   subject-verb agreement
3.   pronoun agreement
4.   articles
5.   prepositions
6.   sentence boundaries

VOCABULARY

1.   Have you used comparison-contrast vocabulary to structure your paragraph?
2.   Have you checked difficult words for correct spelling?

11

PERSONAL OPINION

PREWRITING STRATEGIES

- Is space exploration worthwhile? Why or why not?

- Do you believe there may be life on other planets? Support your answer.

- Imagine that higher life forms than man existed in the universe. What would they be like?

Useful vocabulary for discussion:

outer space
to explore
exploration
astronaut
alien (life form)
science fiction
to revolve
planet
Earth, Mars, Venus, Saturn (and other planets)
sun
star
moon
space colony
to colonize
galaxy
flying saucer
UFO
space capsule
spaceship
interplanetary

Reading Selection

The following is a personal opinion paragraph that discusses the possibilities of life existing on other planets.

living things	I believe there really are green men from Mars or creatures° with brains twice the size of ours living on other planets in the
going around	universe. The earth is just one of many planets revolving° around
endless	our sun, which is only one of an infinite° number of stars in the galaxy. In my opinion, there is no reason to doubt that life exists elsewhere in the universe. Scientists believe they may one day find life on other planets, and to that end, they continuously send out radio waves to communicate with these life forms and send
space explorers	astronauts° and space capsules to explore outer space. Science-fiction writers have created thousands of alien worlds for us in novels, comic strips, TV programs, and movies. Furthermore, if we look at the science fiction of yesterday, we see it has become
identical offspring created from one parent	today's reality. Men on the moon, clones°, and test-tube babies all reflect the hope that life does indeed exist on other planets.

Discussion Questions

1. How do you think "people" on other planets might look? How might they be different from us? How could we explain these differences?

2. Have you ever read a science-fiction novel or seen a science-fiction movie or program (such as *Star Trek* or *Star Wars*)? Discuss the way life on other planets was portrayed.

3. Due to overpopulation on earth, people may one day be forced to colonize the moon or neighboring inhabitable planets. Would you be willing to move to a space frontier? What conditions would be necessary to make life possible for twentieth-century humans on other planets?

WRITING EXERCISES

Organization: Personal Opinion

Here is a list of words and phrases that signal personal opinion.

in my opinion
from my point of view
in my view
it seems to me that
it is clear (to me) that
I think
I believe
I suppose
I agree, I disagree
I am certain, I am sure
I consider
I conclude that
I am positive
I assume
I base my opinion on

Exercise 1

Here is the Reading Selection again. Study it and underline all words and phrases that indicate personal opinion.

I believe there really are green men from Mars or creatures with brains twice the size of ours living on other planets in the universe. The earth is just one of many planets revolving around our sun, which is only one of an infinite number of stars in the galaxy. In my opinion, there is no reason to doubt that life exists elsewhere in the universe. Scientists believe they may one day find life on other planets, and to that end, they continuously send out radio waves to communicate with these life forms and send astronauts and space capsules to explore outer space. Science-fiction writers have created thousands of

Copyright © 1983 by Harcourt Brace Jovanovich, Inc. All rights reserved.

alien worlds for us in novels, comic strips, TV programs, and movies. Furthermore, if we look at the science fiction of yesterday, we see it has become today's reality. Men on the moon, clones, and test-tube babies all reflect the hope that life does indeed exist on other planets.

Exercise 2: Values Clarification

a. Read the problem and study the facts.
b. Decide on your opinion. Should Anne major in art or computer programming?
c. Fill in the outlne below with your opinion stated in the topic sentence, some details for your discussion, and a conclusion restating your opinion.

PROBLEM:

Anne Carpenter is a student at City College. She cannot decide whether to major in art, which shes loves, or computer programming, which is more practical.

FACTS:

Anne is a talented artist.
She has loved to draw and paint since early childhood.
The art field is both limited and competitive.
If Anne is very lucky, she may find a job in advertising.
Anne needs to support herself when she graduates.
There are many jobs for computer programmers.
Computer specialists make good money.
Although Anne receives As in her computer courses, she finds them boring.
Anne will probably marry her boyfriend, Rick, when she graduates.

I.   (Topic Sentence) _____

        _____

        _____

II.   (Discussion)

        A. _____

        _____

Copyright © 1983 by Harcourt Brace Jovanovich, Inc. All rights reserved.

B. _____

_____

C. _____

_____

III. (Conclusion) _____

_____

_____

Exercise 3

MODEL PARAGRAPH: Study the following personal-opinion paragraph. Underline the topic sentence. Circle all words and phrases
that signal personal opinion.

I strongly disagree with the use of capital punishment
as a penalty for certain crimes. From my point of view, the
idea that people can judge one another fairly is unrealis-
tic. It is too easy to misinterpret evidence or allow personal
prejudices to influence one's judgment. There have been
cases where a person was sentenced to death, executed,
and later declared innocent of the accused crime. Such
horrible mistakes are bound to happen. In addition, by
giving a sentence of death to a criminal, society is actually
saying that the person has no value as a human being and
can in no way change. And probably most important is the
"crime" inherent to capital punishment: How can society
condemn a person for murder and then turn around and
repeat the act? For these reasons I believe capital punishment is not a justifiable penalty (in courts of justice).

Exercise 4

Write a personal opinion paragraph on one of the following topics:

Copyright © 1983 by Harcourt Brace Jovanovich, Inc. All rights reserved.

1. Exercise 2 (Values Clarification): Should Anne major in art or computer programming?

2. Should the United States have a compulsory or volunteer army?

3. Should a person be forced to retire at a certain age such as 65?

Fill in the outline below with your topic sentence, some details to be used in your discussion, and your conclusion. Study the list of personal-opinion vocabulary before writing, and try to use some in your paragraph.

I. (Topic Sentence) _____

    _____

    _____

II. (Discussion)

    A. _____

    _____

    B. _____

    _____

    C. _____

    _____

III. (Conclusion) _____

    _____

    _____

Development: Coherence of the Paragraph

In the personal-opinion paragraph, the opinion is stated clearly in the topic sentence. Each of the paragraphs below have confusing topic sentences. The writer has used personal opinion phrases, but has used the words "this" and "that" in place of actual opinion. It is impossible for the reader to know what the writer's idea is. Read each paragraph and write a good topic sentence that expresses the personal opinion developed in the paragraph on the lines provided.

Copyright © 1983 by Harcourt Brace Jovanovich, Inc. All rights reserved.

1. I do not think that is true. Although many people rely on the television news for information about the current world situation, the programs do not inform the public enough in order for them to understand what is happening. If the news in a half-hour television broadcast were written down, it would fill only one and a half columns in a newspaper. On the other hand, newspapers and magazines go into detail and give much more background and information to the reader. I believe that those who insist that television news is a good substitute for the daily newspaper are probably lazy and do not want to take time to read.

_____

_____

_____

2. I agree strongly with this statement. Teenagers are too young to make such important far-reaching decisions. Most of them do not really know what love really is. Also, they are unable to support themselves or a family because they have no training or education yet. In my opinion they should wait until they finish school and have some work experience. Moreover, I think they should date different people before deciding on marriage so they know what type of person they are looking for.

_____

_____

_____

Sentence Combining

Combine each group of sentences to make one sentence. After you combine each sentence, write it on the lines below. The sentences will then make a personal opinion paragraph. The vocabulary cues at the right will help you combine the sentences.

1.   **a.** I think this.
         b. Most people do not have enough respect for   (that)
             their bodies.   (and)
         c. Most people do not have enough respect for
             their physical development.

Copyright © 1983 by Harcourt Brace Jovanovich, Inc. All rights reserved.

2. **a.** Many of us allow ourselves to become lazy.   (and)
    b. Many of us allow ourselves to become out of   (because)
        shape.
    c. We do not get enough exercise.

3. **a.** We could be taking a brisk walk.   (when)
    b. We could be playing a sport on a sunny day.   (or)
    c. We sit in front of the television.

4. **a.** We let years go by without developing a regular
        exercise program.
    b. Our bodies will give each of us this.   (if)
    c. We deserve.   (what)

5. **a.** And that is an old body.
    b. And that is a stiff body.
    c. And that is an unhealthy body.

6. **a.** The body is the only machine.   (that)
    b. The machine improves with continued use.

7. **a.** Therefore, we should all develop an active
        lifestyle.   (that or which)
    b. The lifestyle includes a regular exercise
        program.

8. **a.** Even those of us who do not like sports can get
        enough exercise.   (if)
    b. We do not let elevators, escalators, cars, and
        buses take over the function of the body.

9. **a.** In my opinion we all must make an effort to
        maintain a healthy body.   (because)
    b. There is no way to get a new one.   (after)
    c. The original stops working well.

_____

_____

_____

_____

_____

_____

Copyright © 1983 by Harcourt Brace Jovanovich, Inc. All rights reserved.

_____

_____

_____

_____

_____

_____

_____

_____

_____

_____

_____

_____

_____

_____

_____

_____

Proofreading

The following version of the Reading Selection contains twelve mistakes: subject-verb agreement (2), prepositions (2), plurality (2), pronoun agreement (1), possession (1), articles (2), fragments (1), and run-on sentences (1). Find the mistakes and correct them.

1   I believe there really is green men from Mars or creatures

2 with brains twice the size from ours living on other planets in

3 the universe. The earth is just one of many planets revolving

4 around our sun which is just one of an infinite numbers of stars

Copyright © 1983 by Harcourt Brace Jovanovich, Inc. All rights reserved.

5 in the galaxy. In my opinion, there is no reason to doubt that life

6 exist elsewhere in universe. Scientists believe they may one day

7 find life on other planets, and to that end, he continuously send

8 out radio waves. To communicate with these life forms and send

9 astronauts and space capsules to explore outer space. Science

10 fiction writers have created thousand of alien worlds for us in

11 novels, comic strips, tv programs and movies. And if we look in

12 the science fiction of yesterday, we see it has become today

13 reality, men on moon, clones, and test tube babies all reflect the

14 hope that life does indeed exist on other planets.

Copyright © 1983 by Harcourt Brace Jovanovich, Inc. All rights reserved.

FORMAL WRITING

Writing Topics

Choose one of the three topics below or one of your own and write a personal opinion paragraph about the topic. Remember to state your topic sentence in the *introduction*, to develop your *discussion* completely, and to summarize or restate your main idea in the *conclusion*. Try to use the personal opinion vocabulary you have been practicing. If you want, outline the three parts of the paragraph before writing. Write your paragraph on notebook composition paper.

1. Should the superpowers spend millions of dollars on space exploration when problems like poverty and unemployment plague their people?

2. Do you approve of bi-cultural marriage?

3. In the U.S. suicide is a criminal offense. Do you think people have the right to take their own lives if they want to?

Checklist

ORGANIZATION:

1. Is your topic sentence in the introduction?
2. Does the discussion develop and support your topic sentence?
3. Does your conclusion summarize or restate the topic sentence?

GRAMMAR:
Have you checked for errors in the following?

1. verb tense sequence
2. subject-verb agreement
3. pronoun agreement
4. articles
5. prepositions
6. sentence boundaries

VOCABULARY:

1. Have you used personal opinion vocabulary to structure your paragraph?
2. Have you checked difficult words for mistakes?

PHOTO CREDITS

page xii Allen G. Arpadi. **6** © Ruth Orkin. **10** The Bettmann Archive, Inc. **18** Photography by George Bing, Audio-Visual Center, Brooklyn College. **24** © Michael Philip Manheim, 1975/Photo Researchers, Inc. **36** Philadelphia Museum of Art: SmithKline Corporation Collection.
50 Courtesy of Foster & Kleiser. **66** © Mary Eleanor Browning/Photo Researchers, Inc. **78** Bernard Pierre Wolff/Photo Researchers, Inc. **92** Roberta Hershenson/Photo Researchers, Inc. **106** The Bettmann Archive, Inc. **118** Ed Lettan/Photo Researchers, Inc. **132** NASA.

G 9
H 0
I 1
J 2